KEYBOARD
PICTURE CHORDS
IN COLOR

OVER 300 KEYBOARD CHORDS IN FULL COLOR!
THE BEST PICTURE-CHORD BOOK FOR ANY KEYBOARD PLAYER

W9-AAV-976

Cover photograph: © age fotostock/SuperStock
Project editor: Felipe Orozco
Interior design and layout: Len Vogler

This book Copyright © 2006 by Amsco Publications,
A Division of Music Sales Corporation, New York

Order No. AM 982124
ISBN-10: 0.8256.3368.0
ISBN-13: 978.0.8256.3368.3

Exclusive Distributors:
Music Sales Corporation
257 Park Avenue South, New York, NY 10010 USA
Music Sales Limited
14-15 Berners Street, London W1T 3LJ England
Music Sales Pty. Limited
120 Rothschild Street, Rosebery, Sydney, NSW 2018, Australia

Printed in the United States of America by
Vicks Lithograph and Printing Corporation

Amsco Publications
part of the Music Sales Group
New York/Nashville/London/Paris/Sydney/Copenhagen/Berlin/Tokyo/Madrid

Table of Contents

Keyboard Diagram

The diagrams used to illustrate the chords are very easy to read. The 3-D graphic shows what keys are used to make up the chords. The keys are pushed down for both the white and black keys, and shaded in light grey for the black keys. The notes of each chord are located below and above each note. The root of each chord is enclosed in a circle. The name of each chord is located on the upper left side of each photograph; the notation is located on the upper right side.

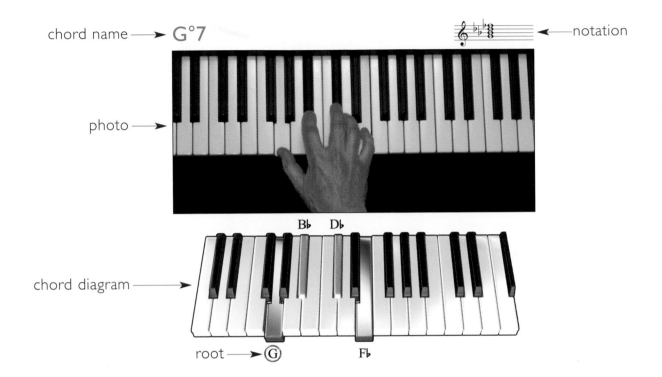

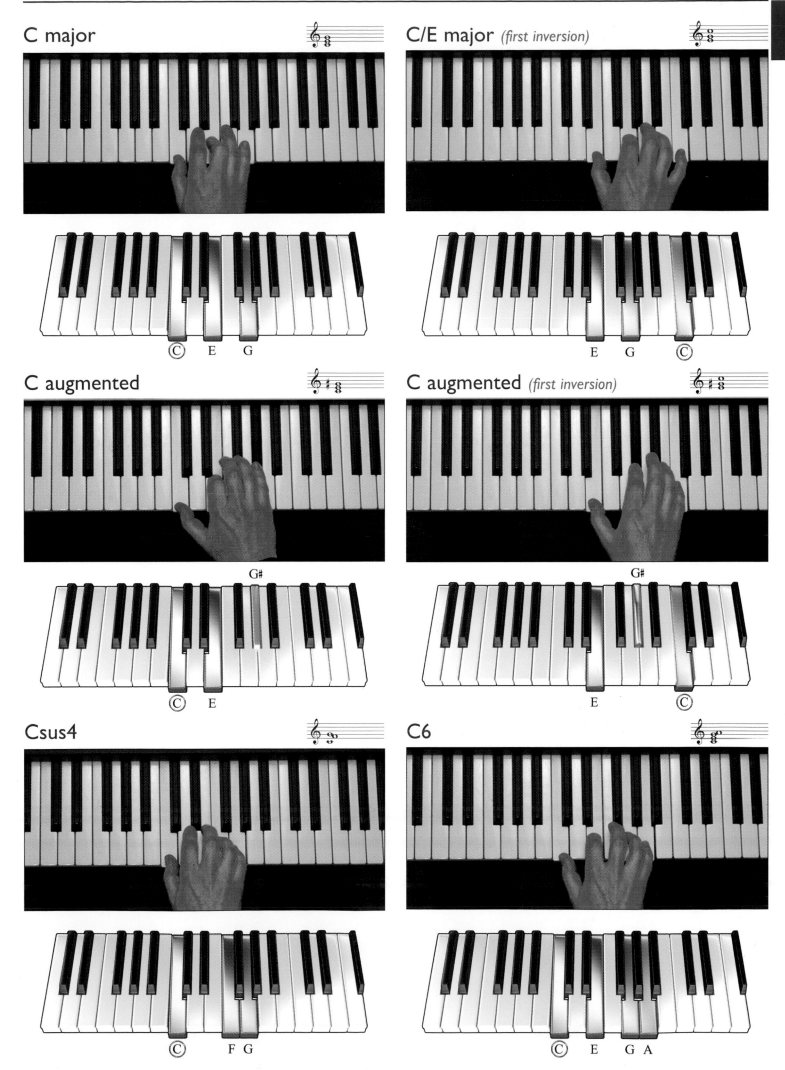

C7

B♭
© E G

C7 (first inversion)

B♭
E G ©

C°7

E♭ G♭
© B♭♭

C°7 (first inversion)

E♭ G♭
B♭♭ ©

C major7

© E G B

C major7 (first inversion)

E G B ©

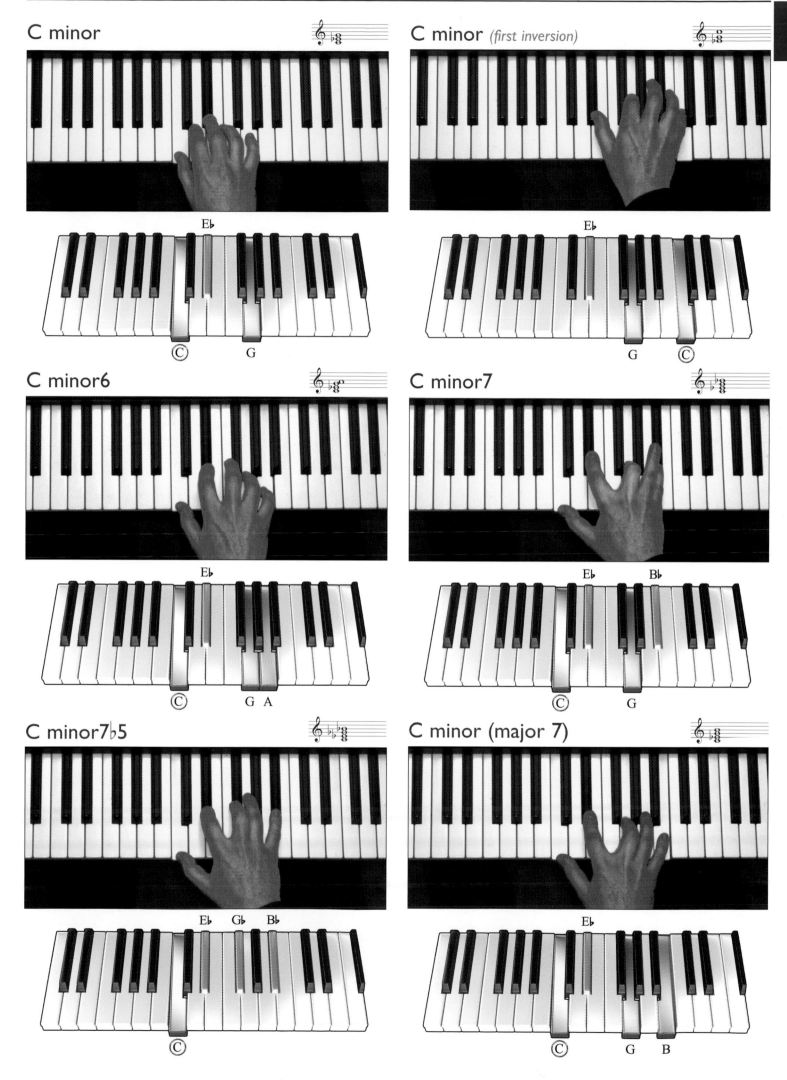

C minor

C minor *(first inversion)*

C minor6

C minor7

C minor7♭5

C minor (major 7)

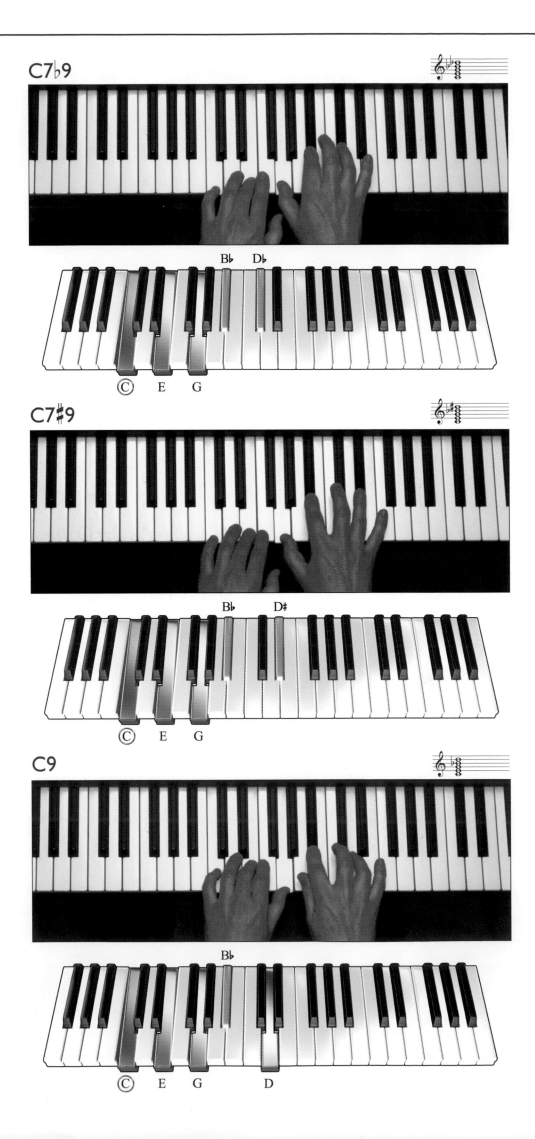

D♭ major

D♭/F major (first inversion)

D♭ — A♭

F

A♭ — D♭

F

D♭ augmented

D♭ augmented (first inversion)

D♭

F   A

D♭

F   A

D♭sus4

D♭6

D♭   G♭ A♭

D♭   A♭ B♭

F

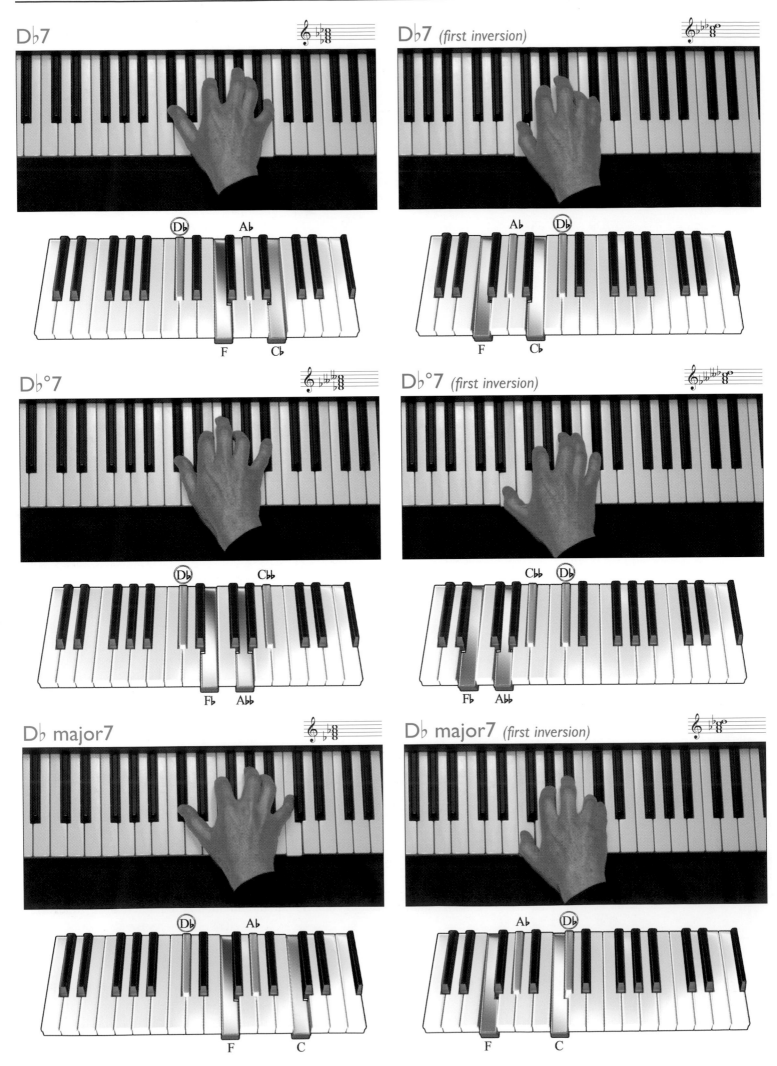

D♭

D♭ minor

D♭　　　A♭

F♭

D♭ minor *(first inversion)*

A♭　　D♭

F♭

D♭ minor6

D♭　　　A♭ B♭

F♭

D♭ minor7

D♭　　　A♭

F♭　　　C♭

D♭ minor7♭5

D♭

F♭　　A♭♭　C♭

D♭ minor (major 7)

D♭　　　A♭

F♭　　　C

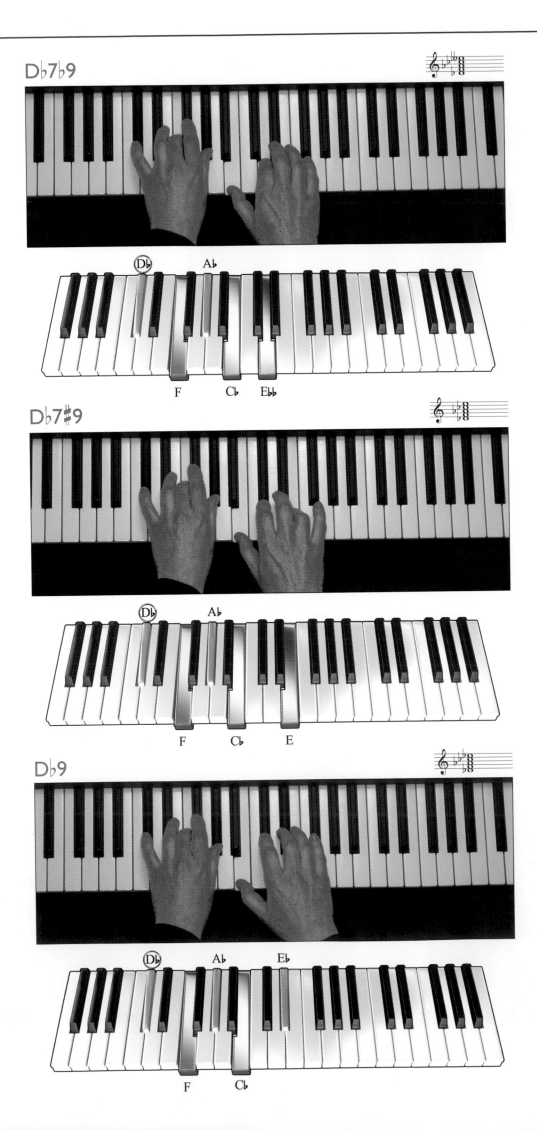

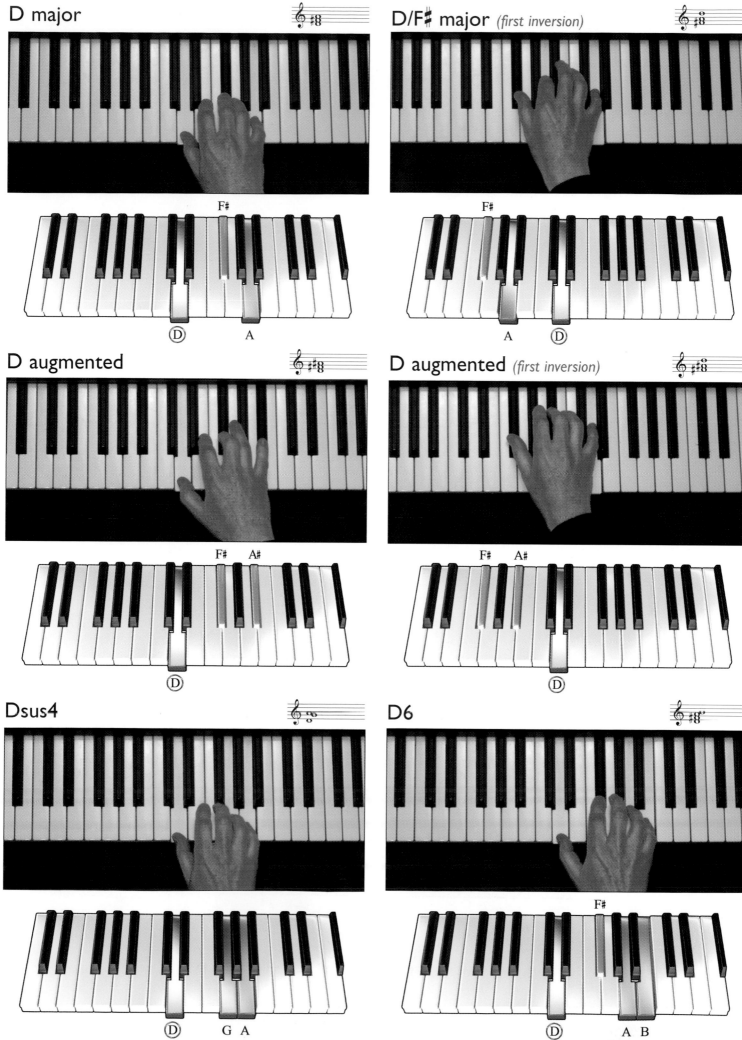

D major

D/F♯ major *(first inversion)*

D augmented

D augmented *(first inversion)*

Dsus4

D6

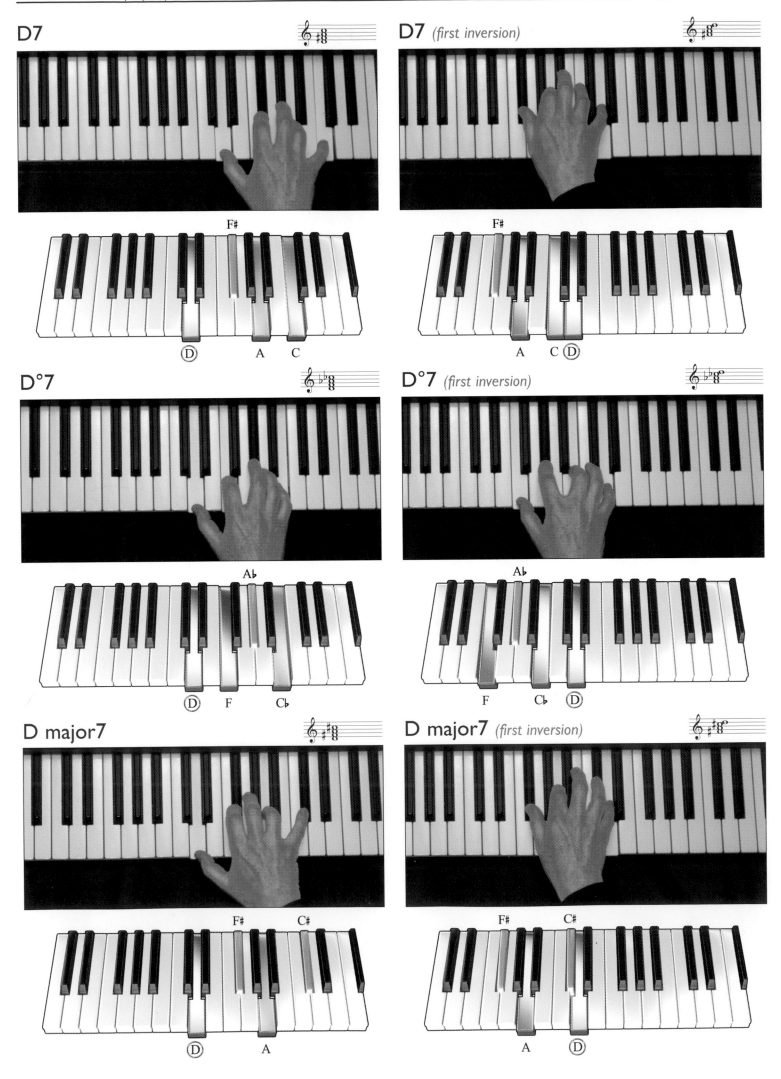

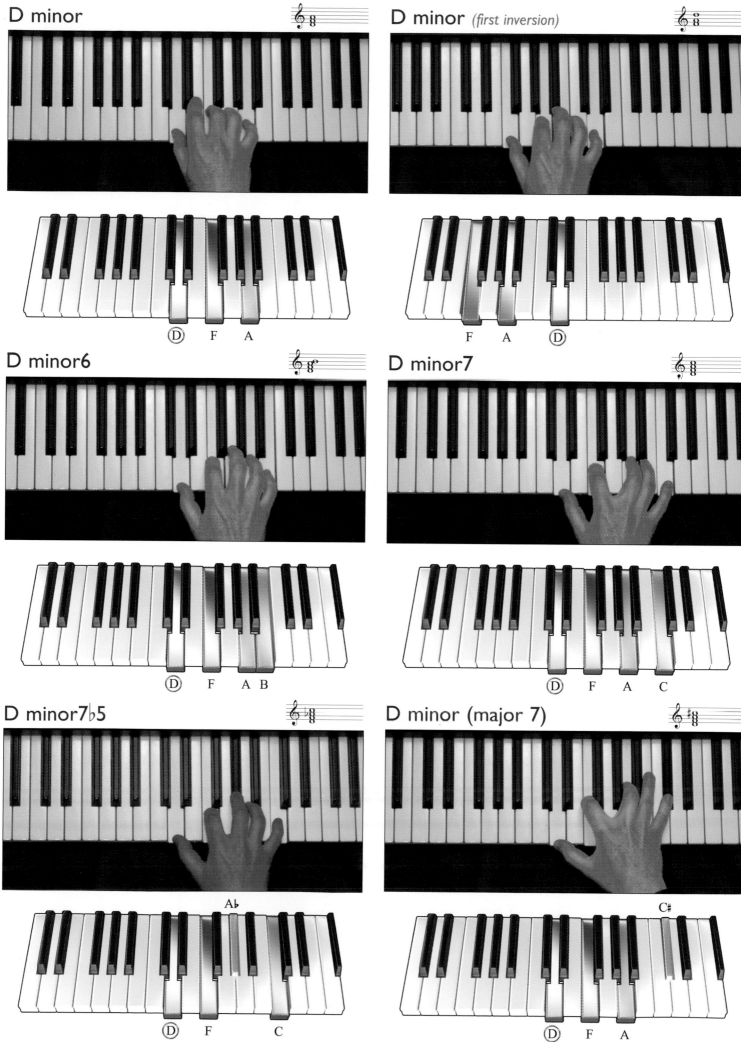

D minor

D minor *(first inversion)*

D A

F A D

D minor6

D minor7

D F A B

D F A C

D minor7♭5

D minor (major 7)

A♭

C#

D F C

D F A

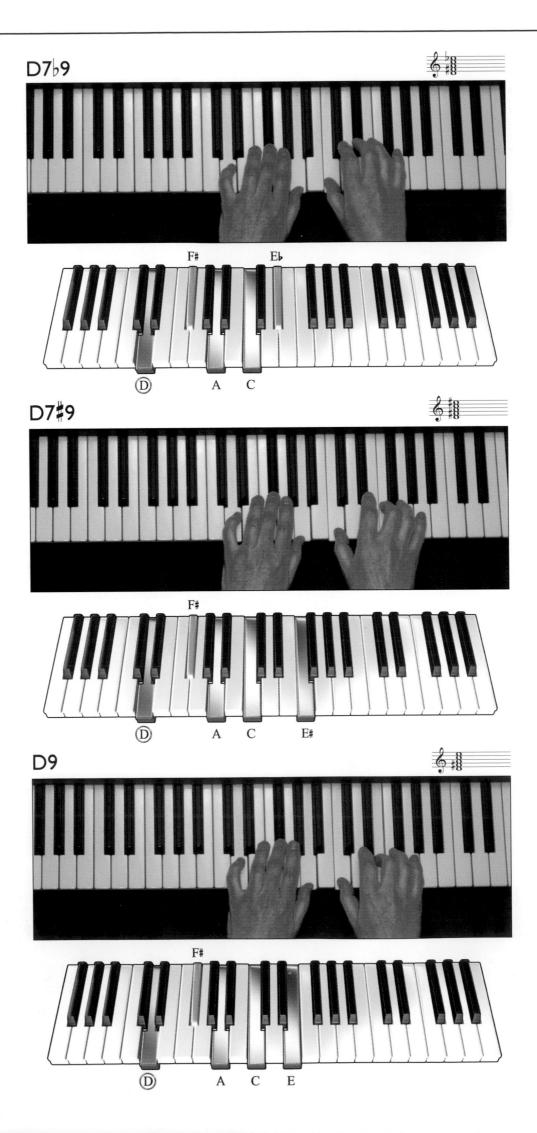

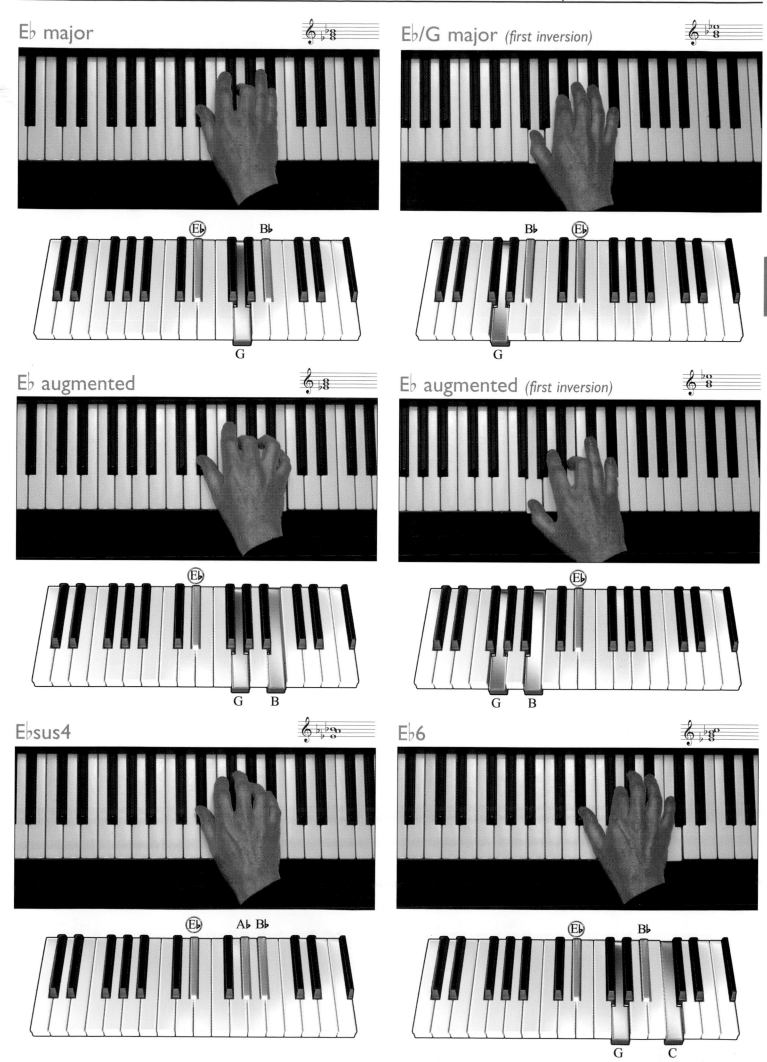

E♭ major

E♭/G major (first inversion)

E♭ augmented

E♭ augmented (first inversion)

E♭sus4

E♭6

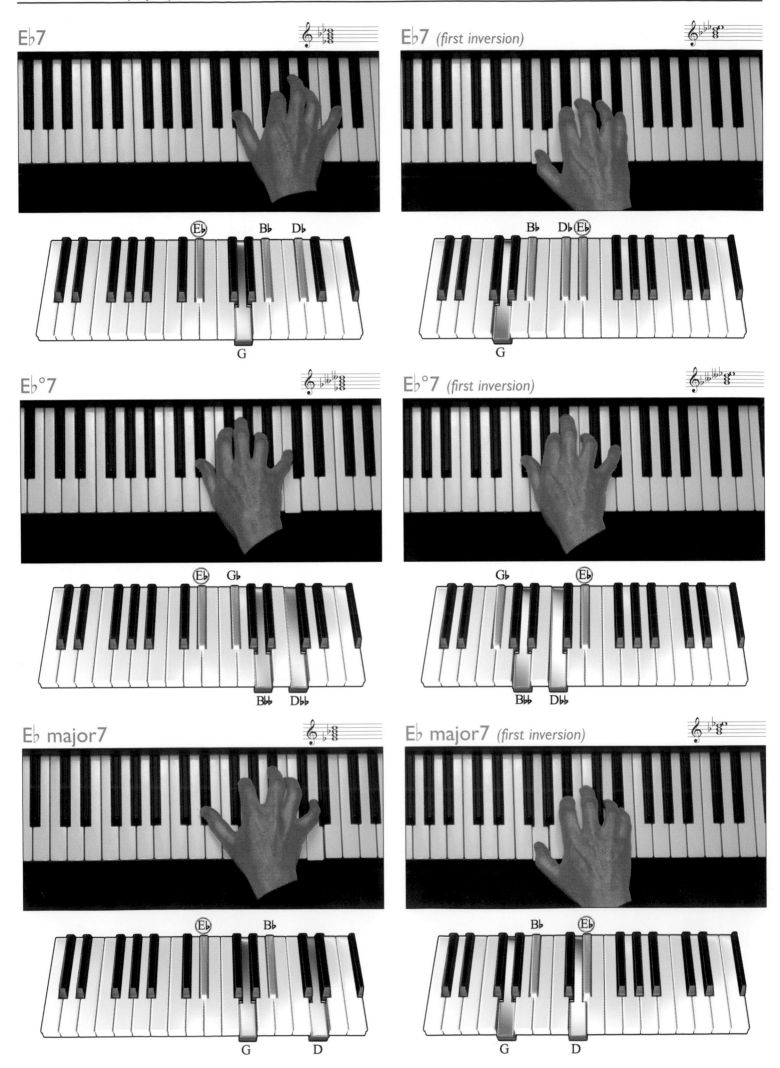

E♭7

E♭7 *(first inversion)*

E♭°7

E♭°7 *(first inversion)*

E♭ major7

E♭ major7 *(first inversion)*

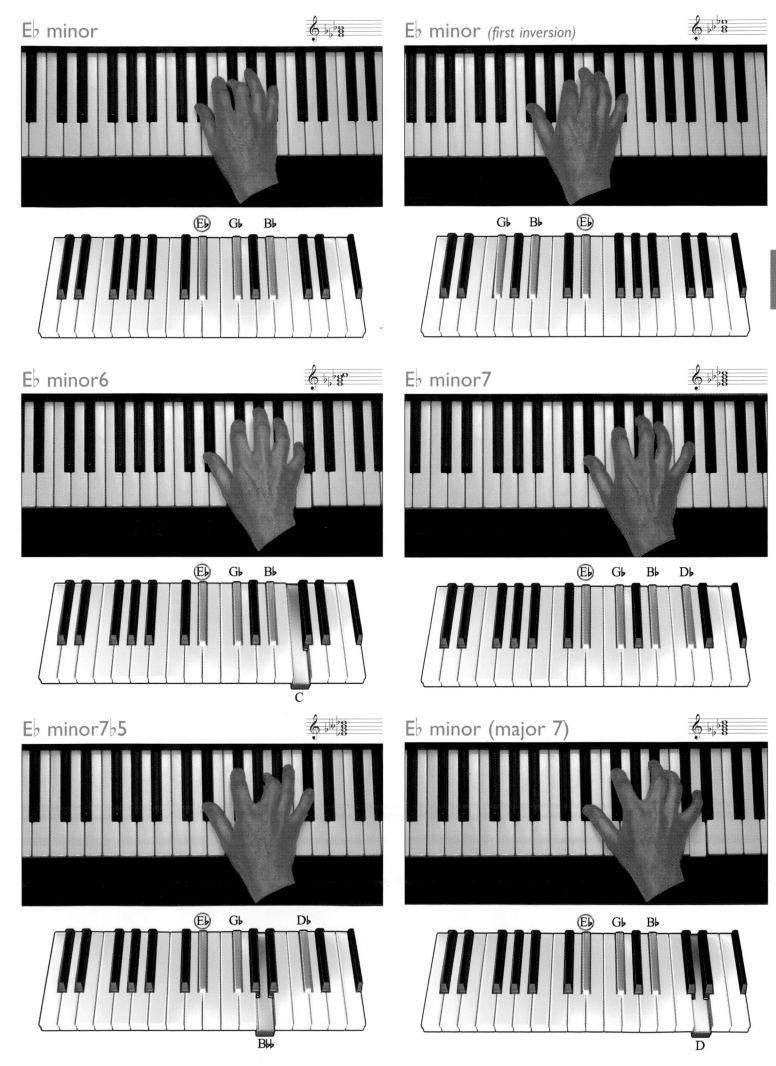

E♭ minor

E♭ minor *(first inversion)*

E♭ minor6

E♭ minor7

E♭ minor7♭5

E♭ minor (major 7)

E♭

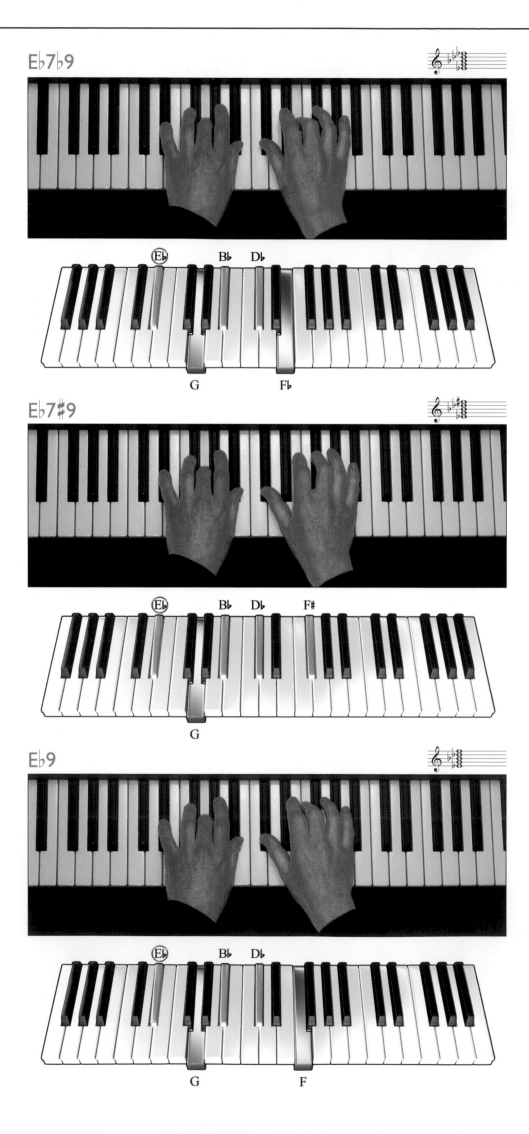

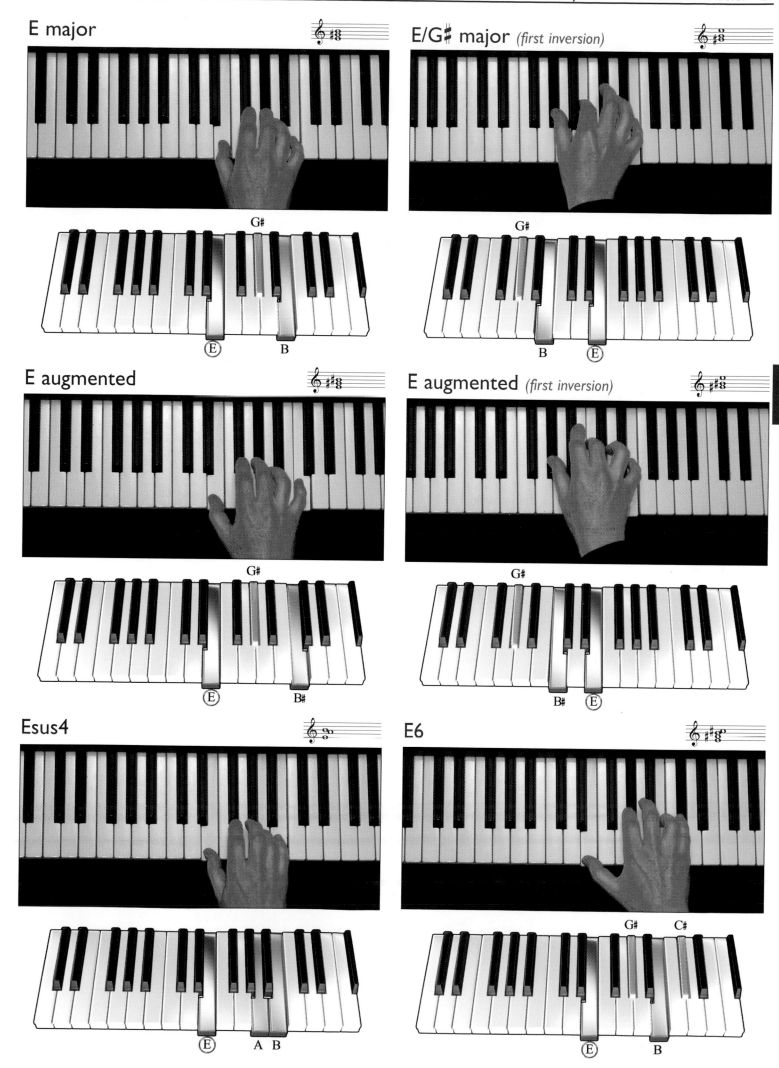

E major

E/G♯ major (first inversion)

E augmented

E augmented (first inversion)

Esus4

E6

E7

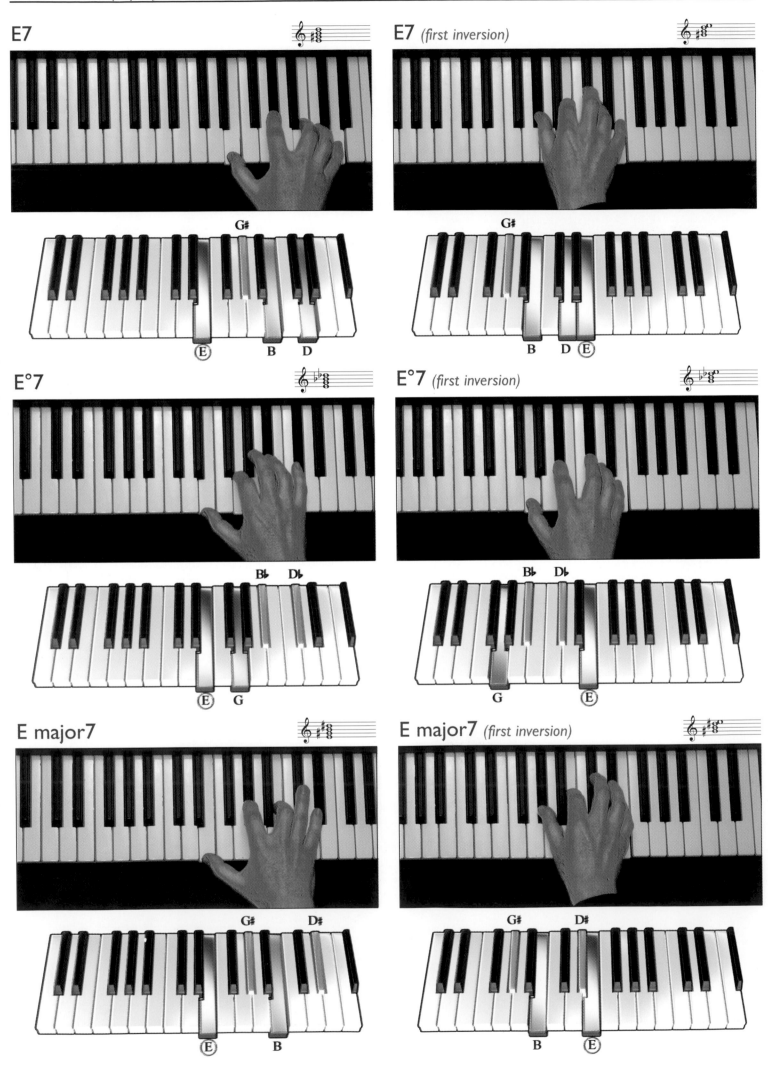

G#

E B D

E7 *(first inversion)*

G#

B D E

E°7

B♭ D♭

E G

E°7 *(first inversion)*

B♭ D♭

G E

E major7

G# D#

E B

E major7 *(first inversion)*

G# D#

B E

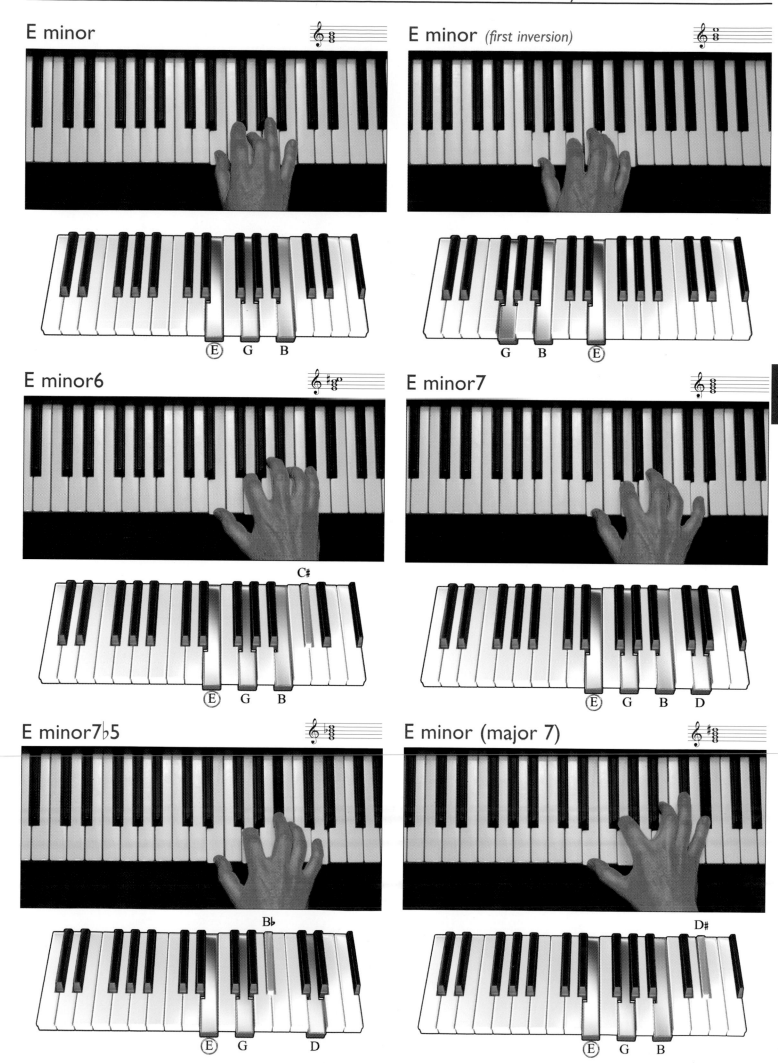

E minor

E G B

E minor *(first inversion)*

G B E

E minor6

E G B C#

E minor7

E G B D

E minor7♭5

E G B♭ D

E minor (major 7)

E G B D#

E

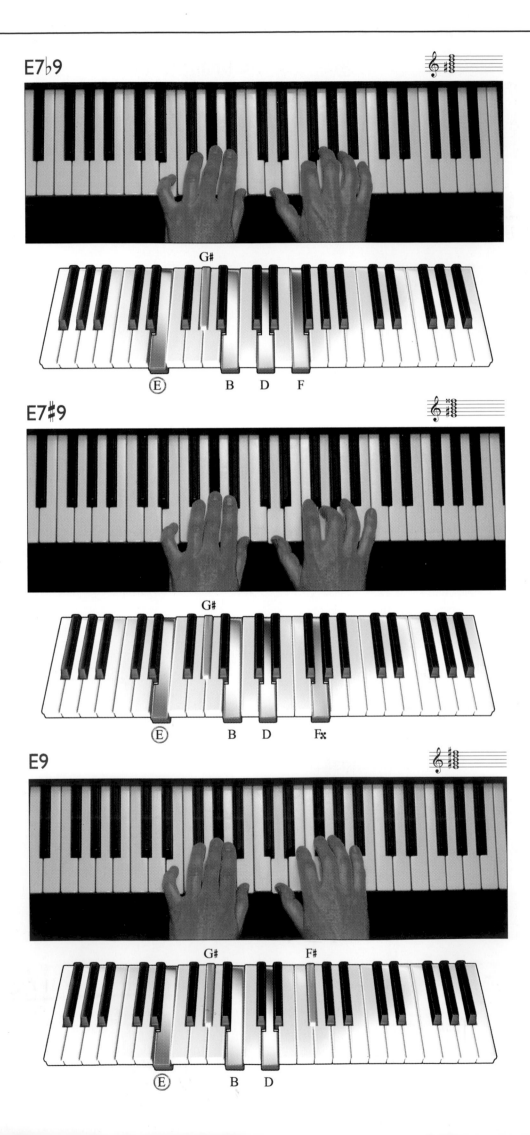

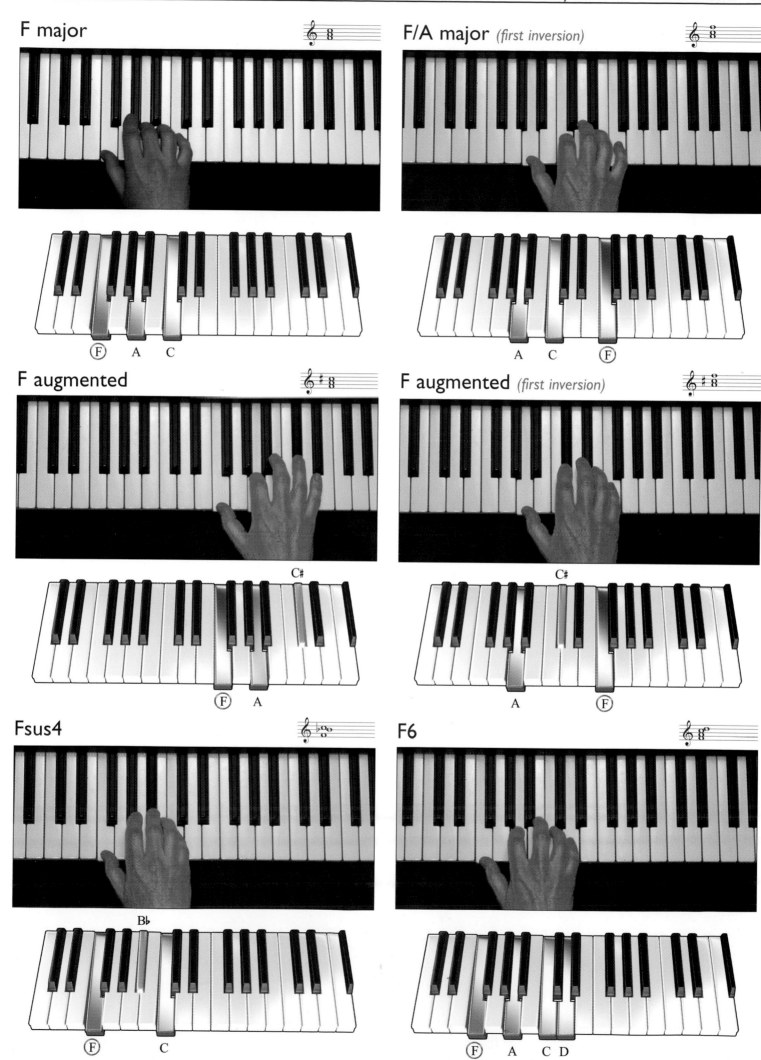

F major

F/A major *(first inversion)*

F A C

A C F

F augmented

F augmented *(first inversion)*

C#

F A

C#

A F

Fsus4

F6

B♭

F C

F A C D

F

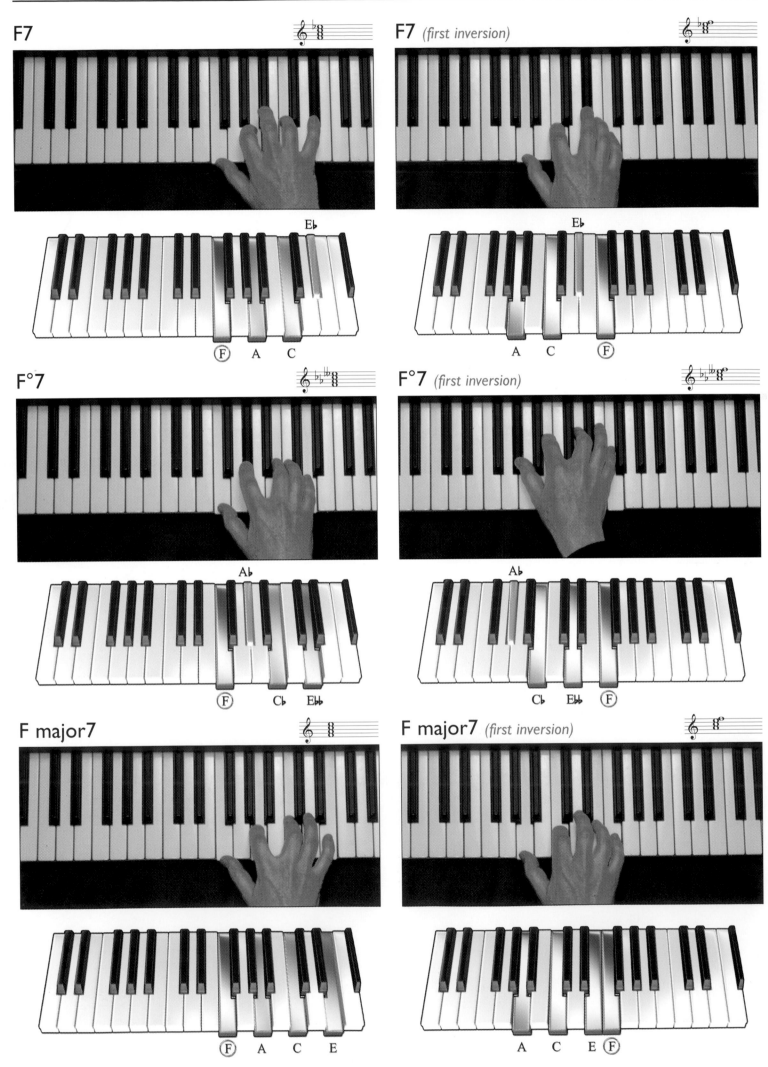

F7

F A C   Eb

F7 *(first inversion)*

A C   F   Eb

F°7

F   Cb   Ebb   Ab

F°7 *(first inversion)*

Cb   Ebb   F   Ab

F major7

F A C E

F major7 *(first inversion)*

A C E F

F minor

F minor *(first inversion)*

F minor6

F minor7

F minor7♭5

F minor (major 7)

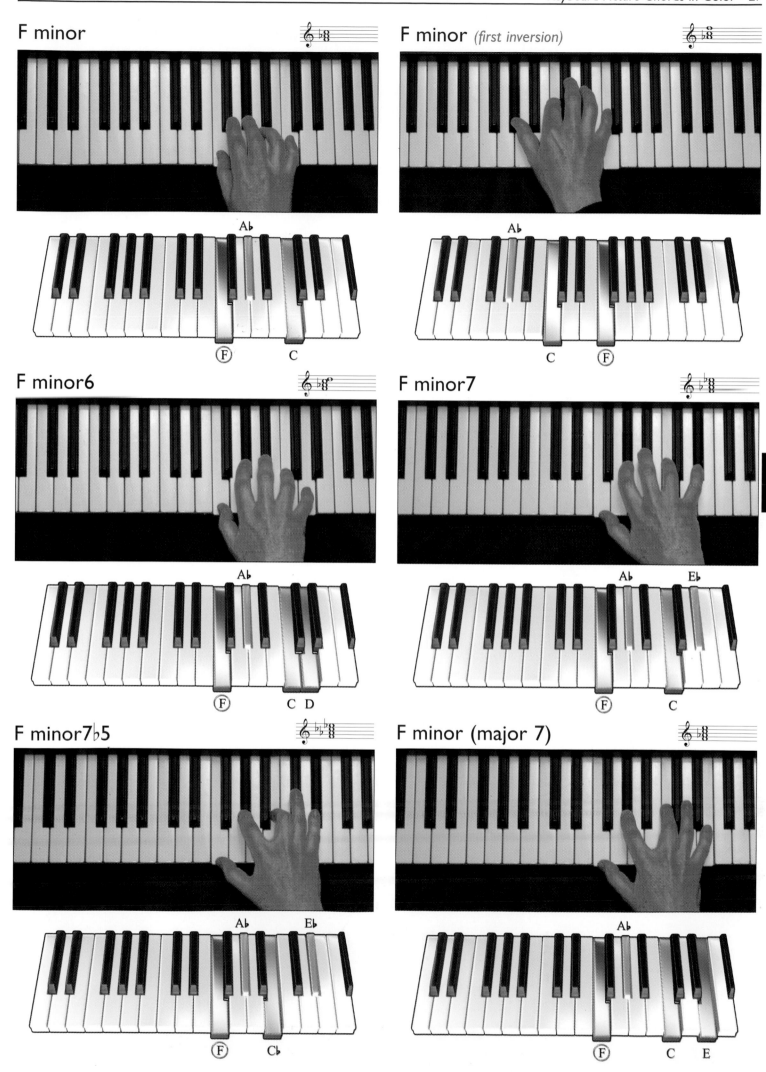

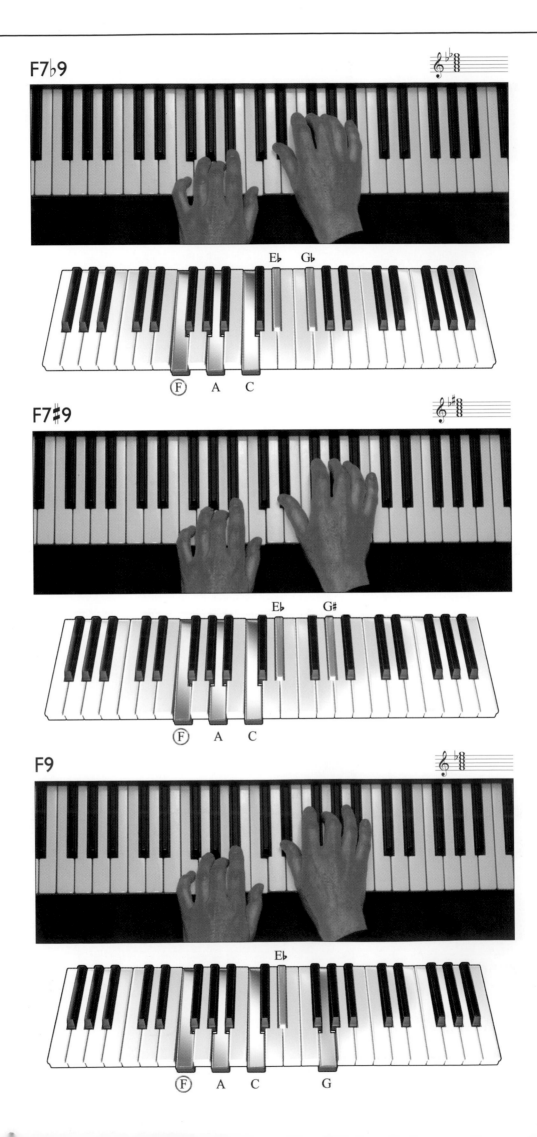

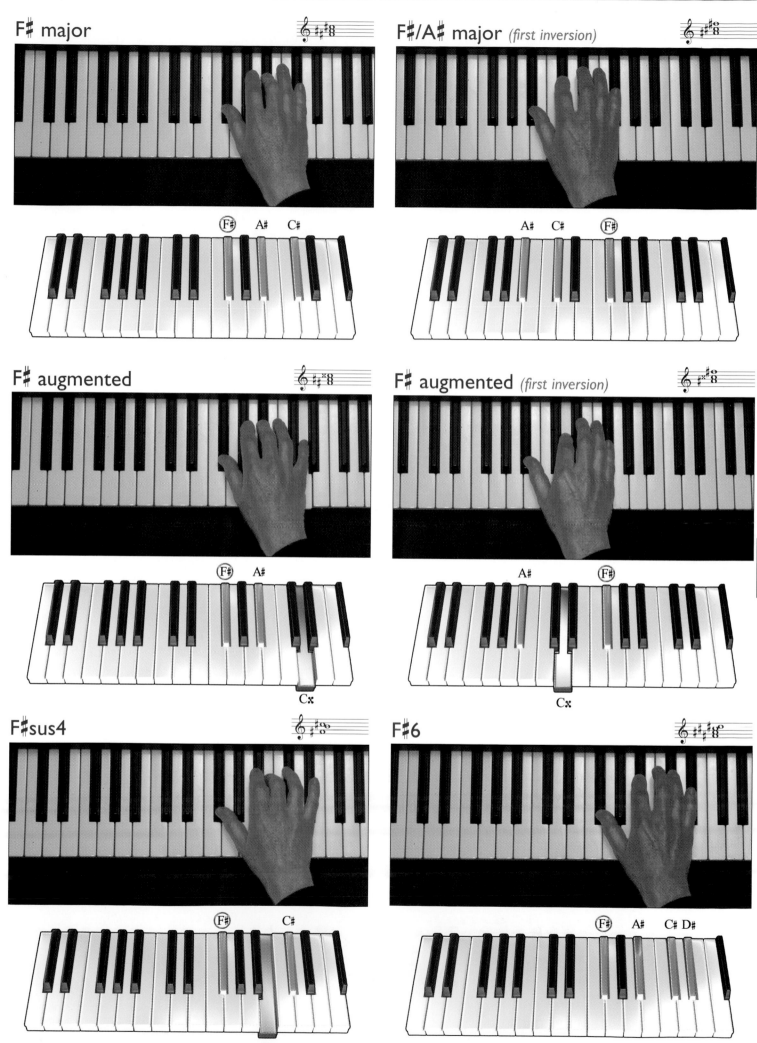

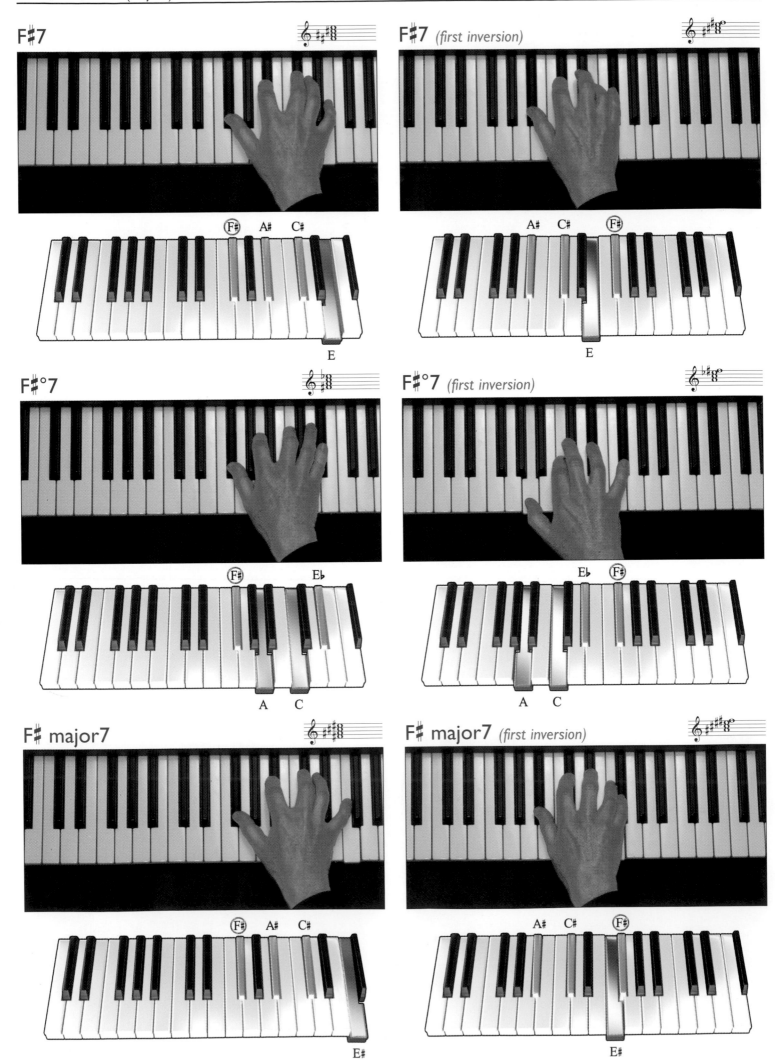

F#7

F#7 (first inversion)

F#°7

F#°7 (first inversion)

F# major7

F# major7 (first inversion)

F# minor

F# minor *(first inversion)*

F# minor6

F# minor7

F# minor7♭5

F# minor (major 7)

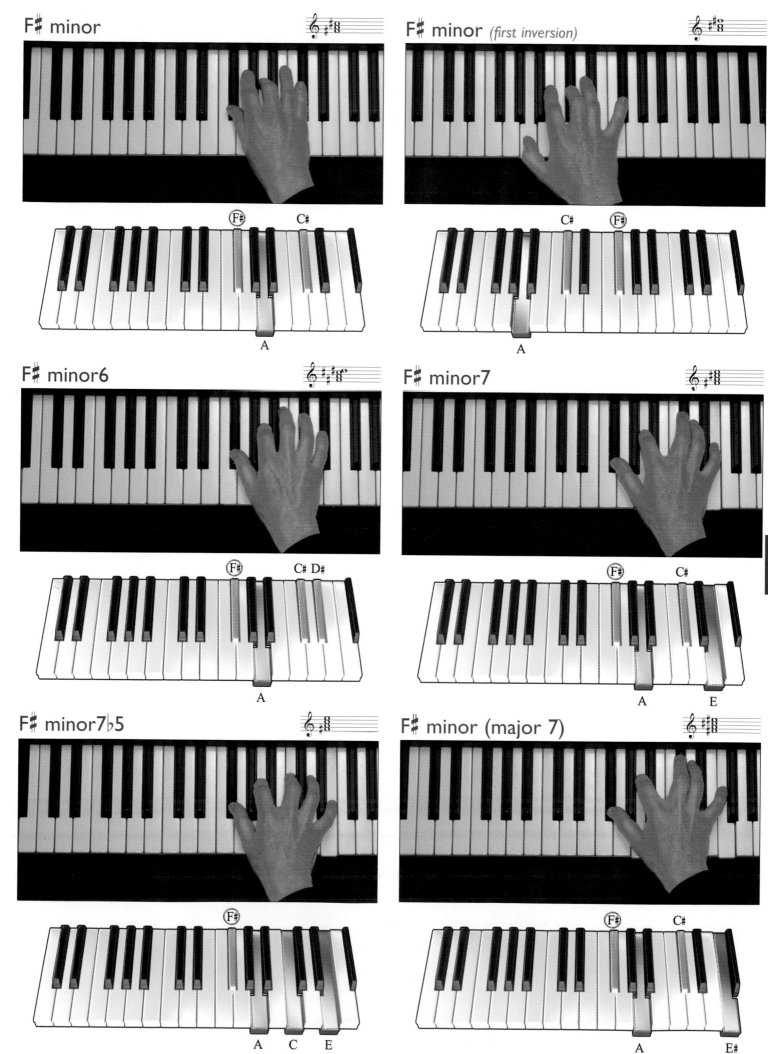

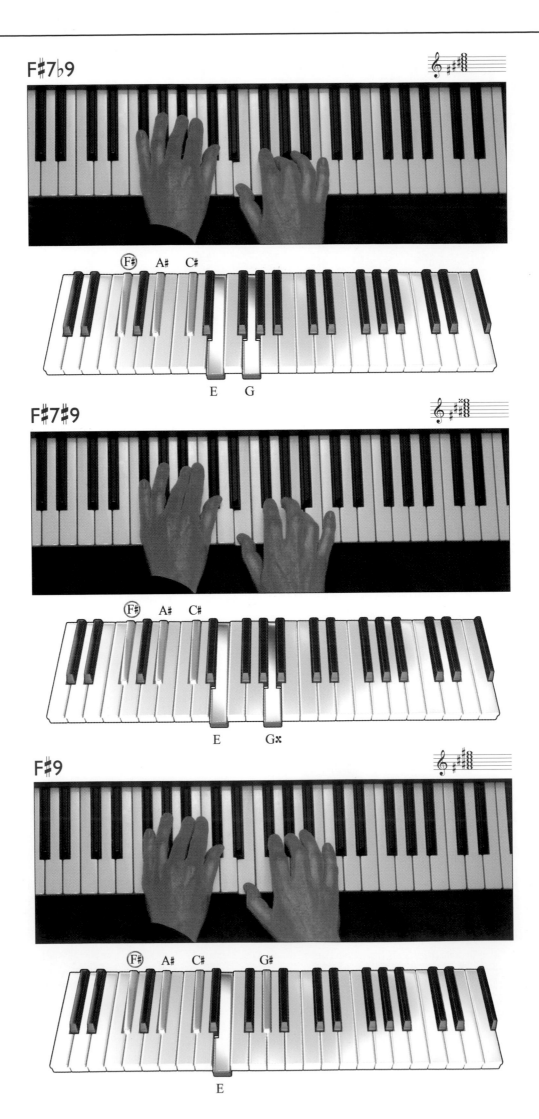

G major

G/B major *(first inversion)*

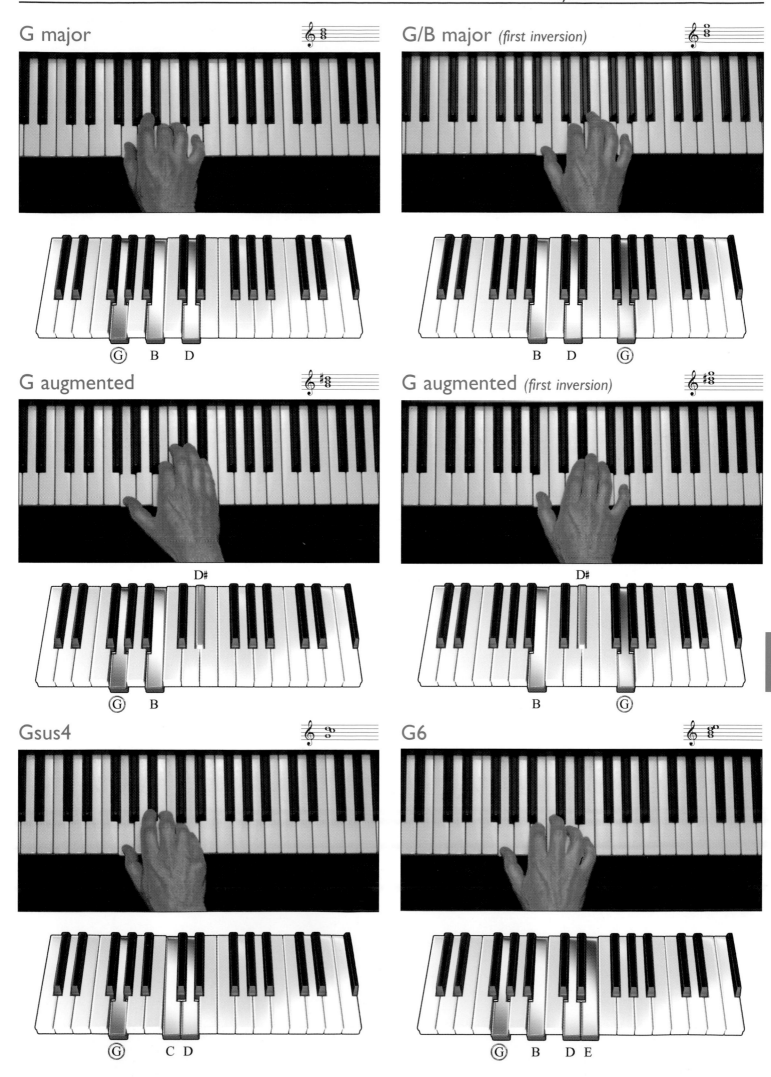

G B D

B D G

G augmented

G augmented *(first inversion)*

D#

D#

G B

B G

Gsus4

G6

G C D

G B D E

G

G7

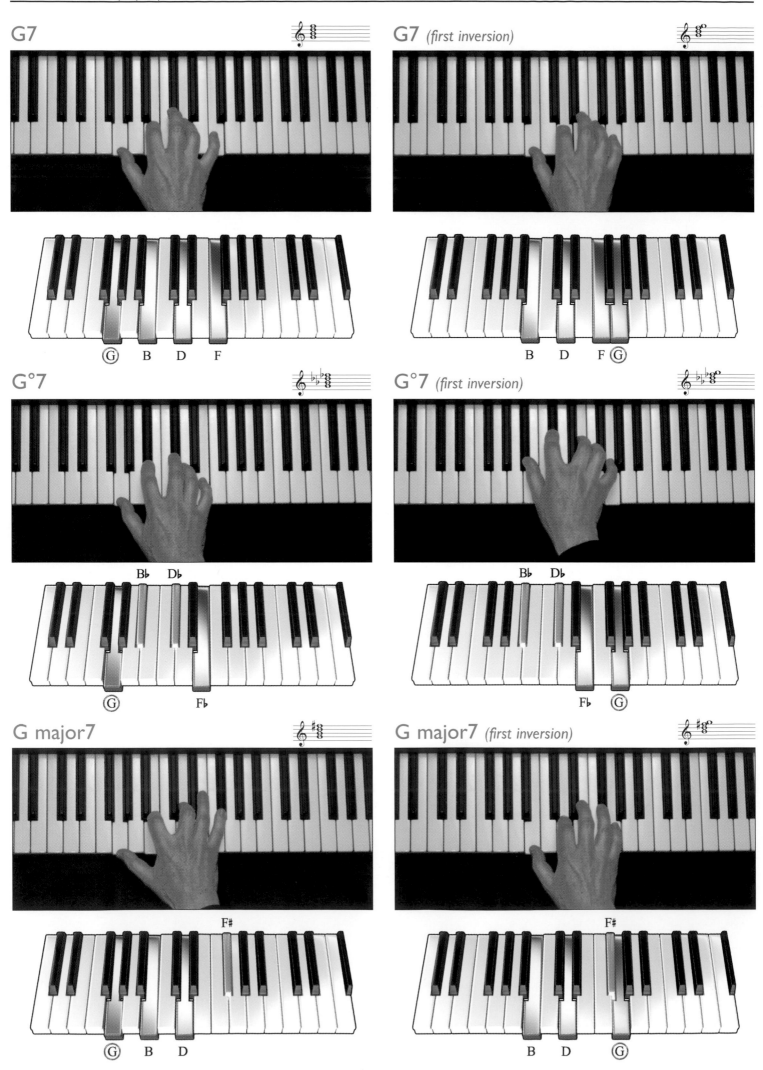

G B D F

G7 *(first inversion)*

B D F G

G°7

B♭ D♭

G F♭

G°7 *(first inversion)*

B♭ D♭

F♭ G

G major7

F#

G B D

G major7 *(first inversion)*

F#

B D G

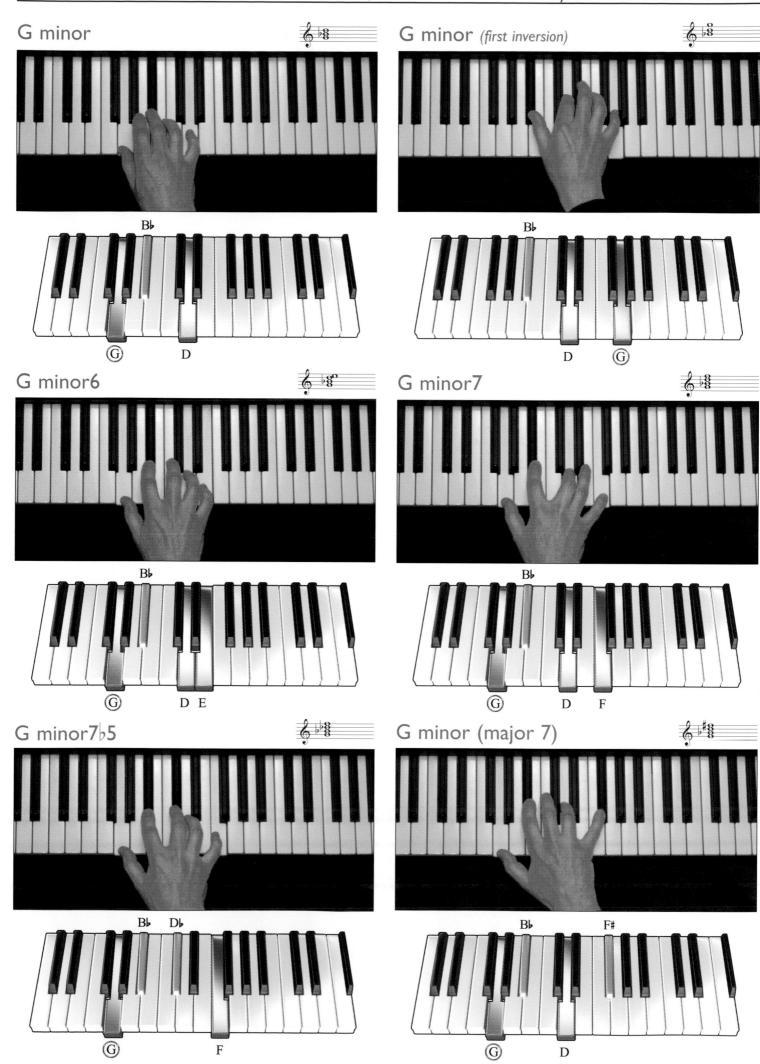

G minor

G minor *(first inversion)*

Bb
G   D

Bb
D   G

G minor6

G minor7

Bb
G   D E

Bb
G   D F

G minor7b5

G minor (major 7)

Bb   Db
G   F

Bb   F#
G   D

G

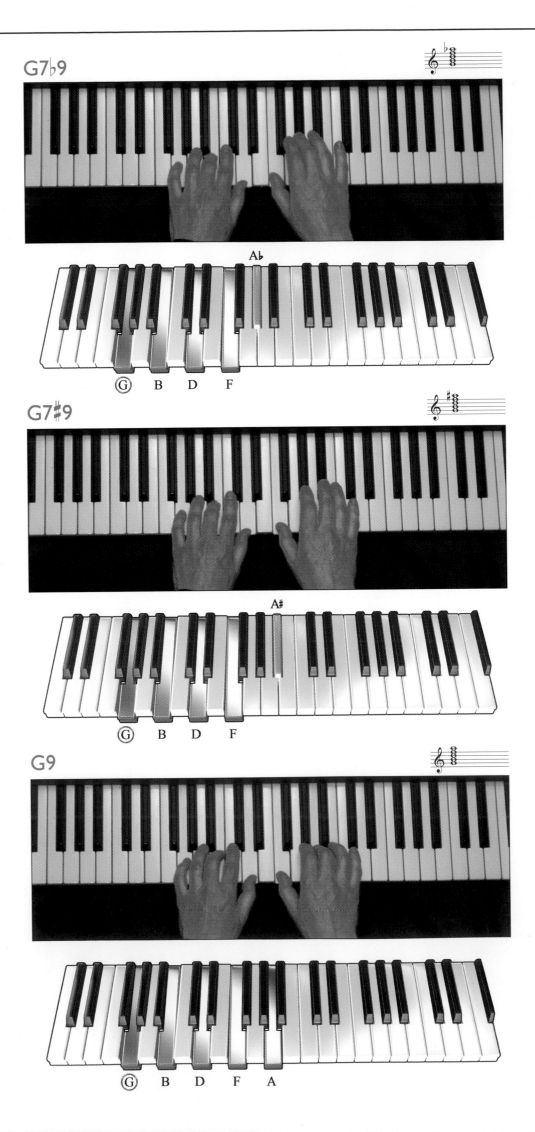

A♭ major

A♭/C major *(first inversion)*

A♭ augmented

A♭ augmented *(first inversion)*

A♭sus4

A♭6

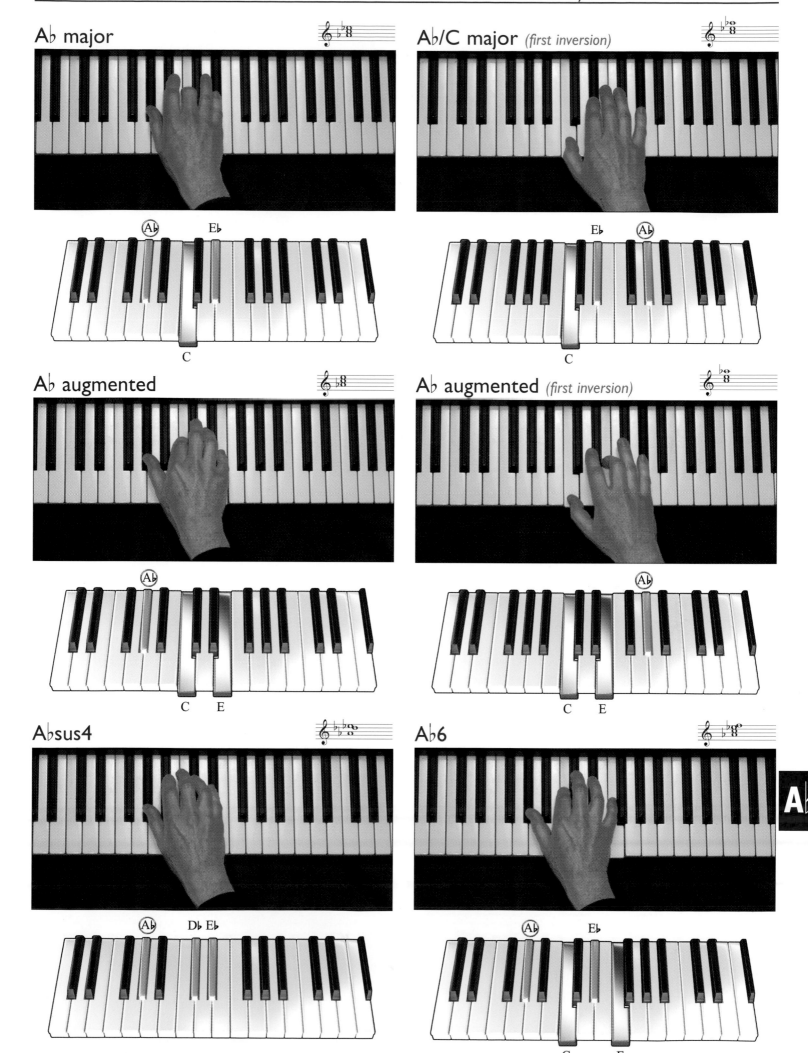

A♭

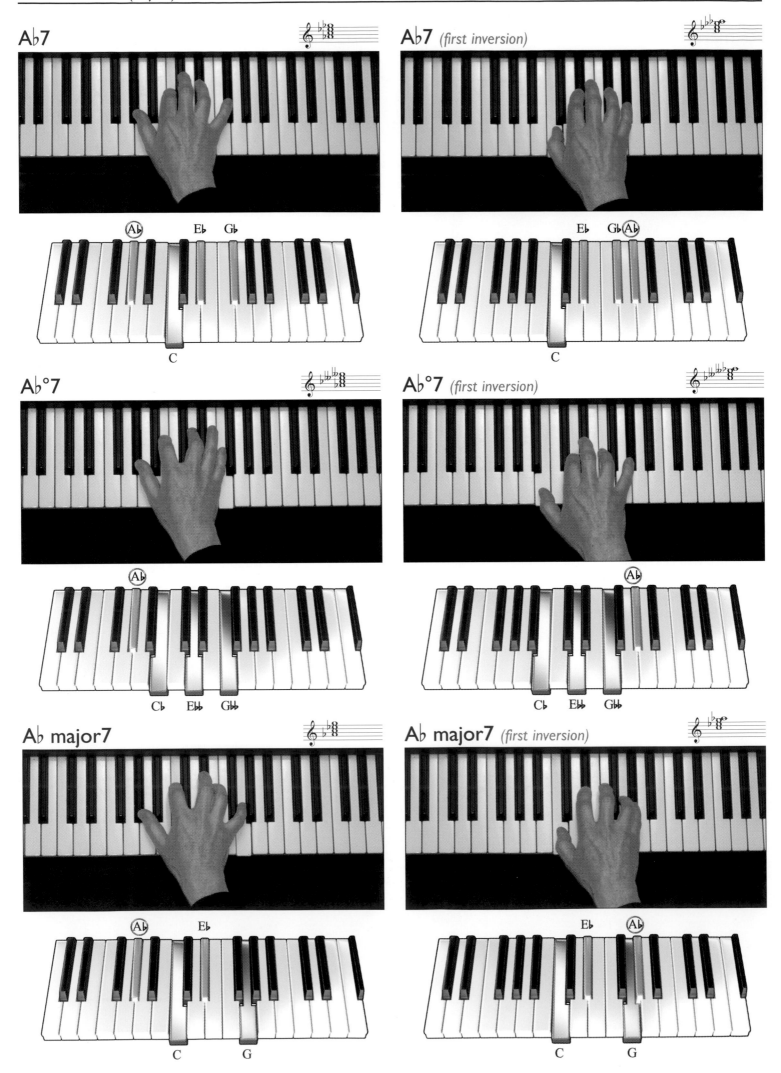

A♭ minor

A♭   E♭

C♭

A♭ minor *(first inversion)*

E♭   A♭

C♭

A♭ minor6

A♭   E♭

C♭   F

A♭ minor7

A♭   E♭   G♭

C♭

A♭ minor7♭5

A♭   G♭

C♭   E♭♭

A♭ minor (major 7)

A♭   E♭

C♭   G

A♭

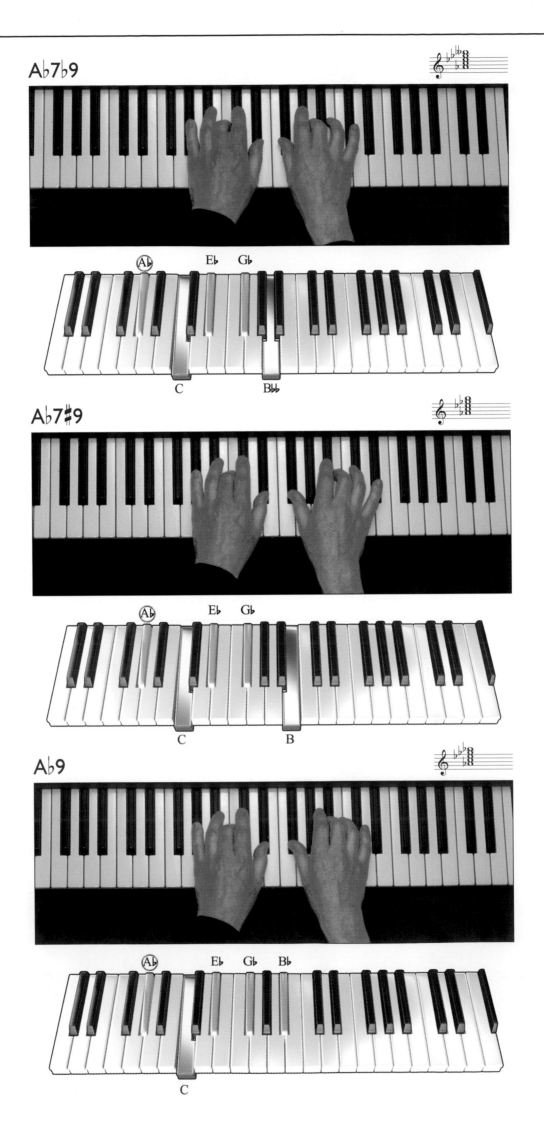

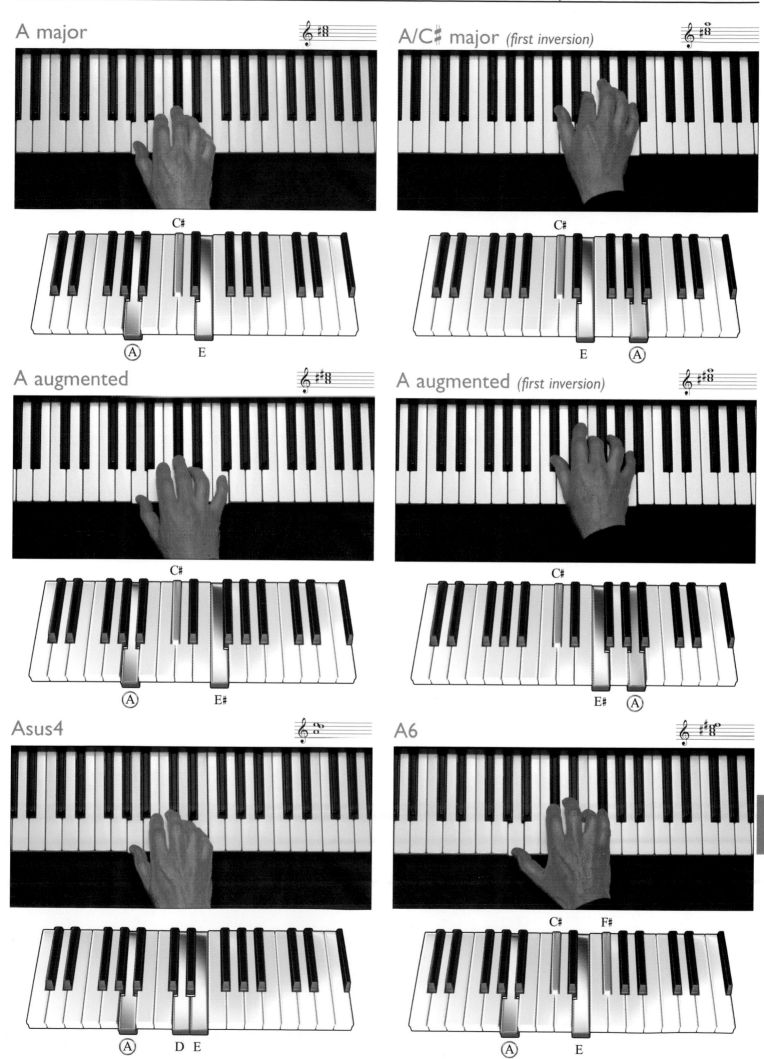

A major

A/C♯ major *(first inversion)*

A augmented

A augmented *(first inversion)*

Asus4

A6

A

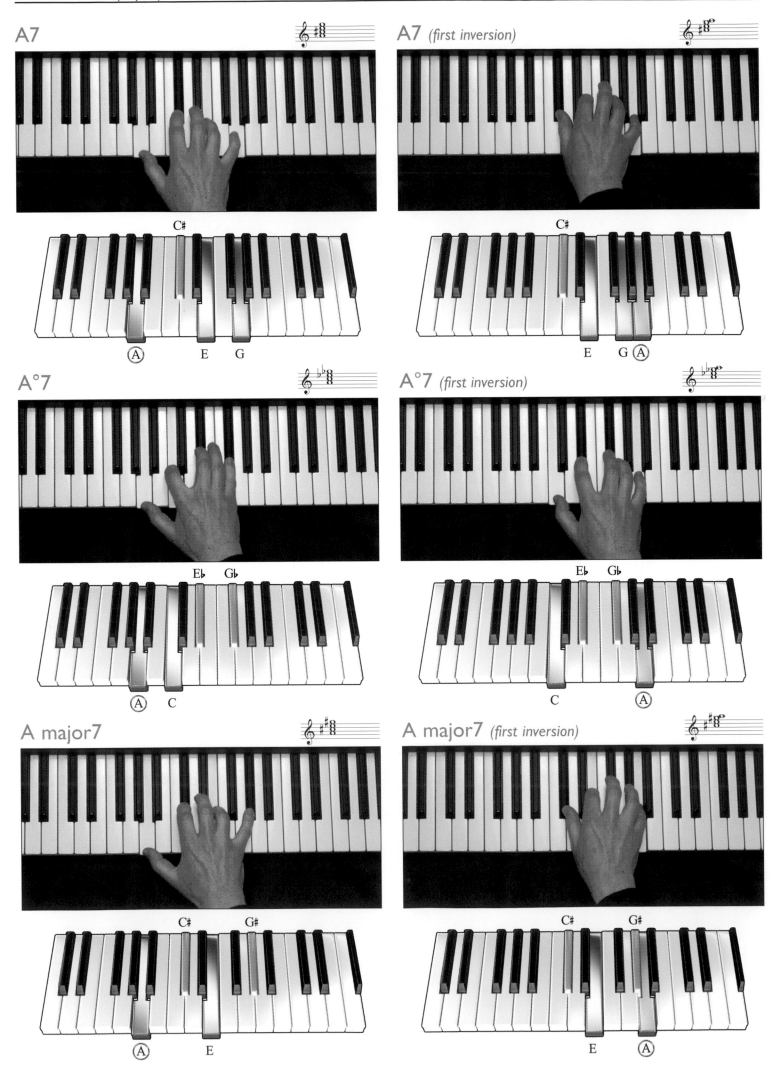

A7

C#

Ⓐ   E   G

A7 (first inversion)

C#

E   G Ⓐ

A°7

E♭   G♭

Ⓐ   C

A°7 (first inversion)

E♭   G♭

C   Ⓐ

A major7

C#   G#

Ⓐ   E

A major7 (first inversion)

C#   G#

E   Ⓐ

A minor

A minor (first inversion)

Ⓐ C E

C E Ⓐ

A minor6

F#

Ⓐ C E

A minor7

Ⓐ C E G

A minor7♭5

E♭

Ⓐ C G

A minor (major 7)

G#

Ⓐ C E

A

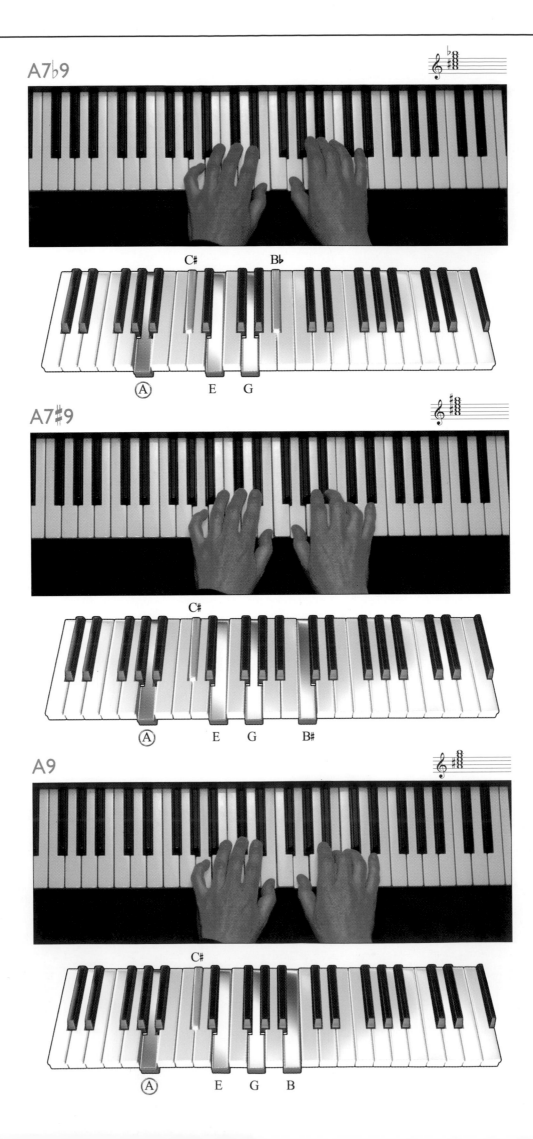

B♭ major

B♭/D major *(first inversion)*

B♭ augmented

B♭ augmented *(first inversion)*

B♭sus4

B♭6

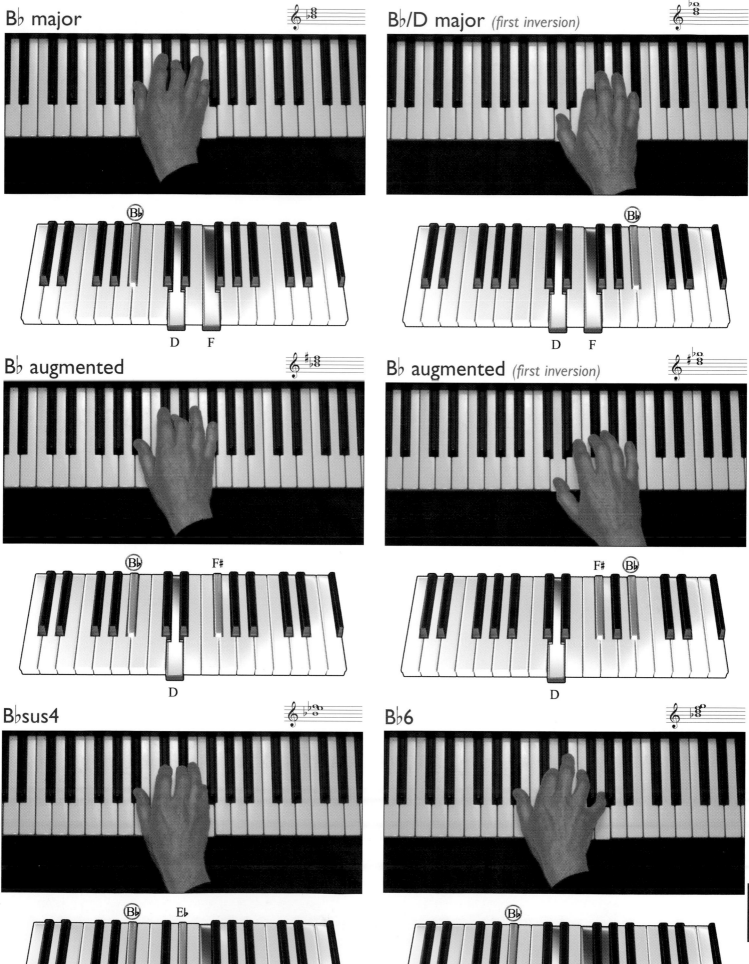

B♭ major: D F

B♭/D major: D F

B♭ augmented: B♭ F# D

B♭ augmented (first inversion): F# B♭ D

B♭sus4: B♭ E♭ F

B♭6: B♭ D F G

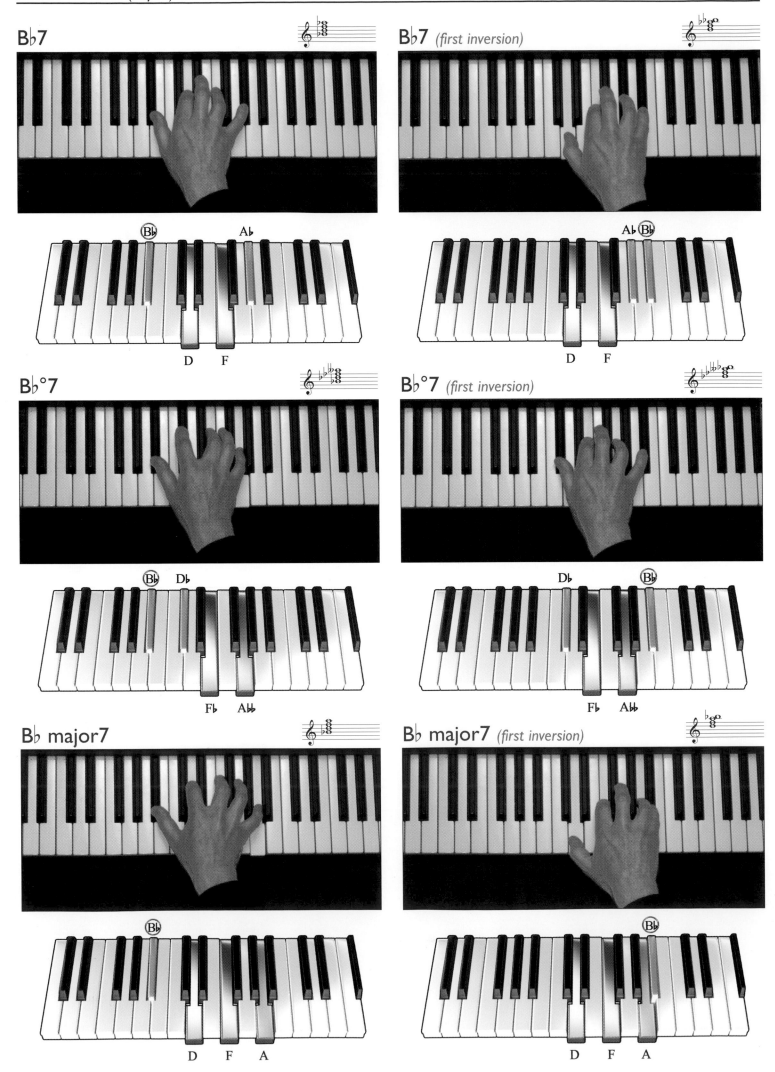

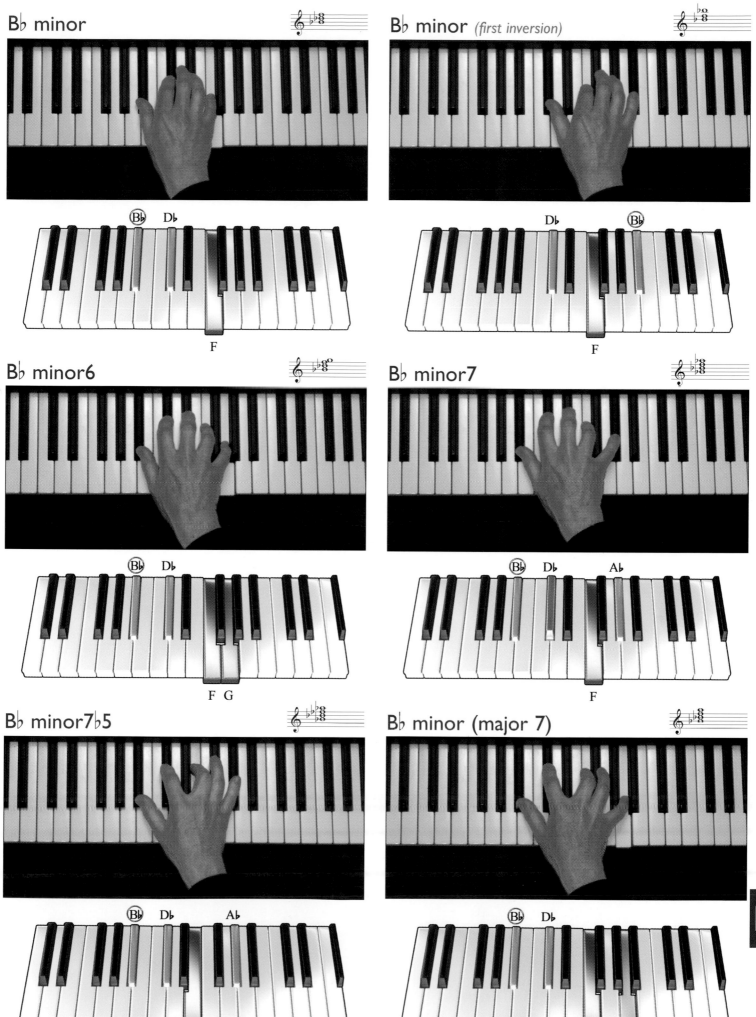

B♭ minor

B♭ minor *(first inversion)*

B♭ B♭ D♭ F

D♭ B♭ F

B♭ minor6

B♭ minor7

B♭ D♭ F G

B♭ D♭ A♭ F

B♭ minor7♭5

B♭ minor (major 7)

B♭ D♭ A♭ F♭

B♭ D♭ F A

B♭

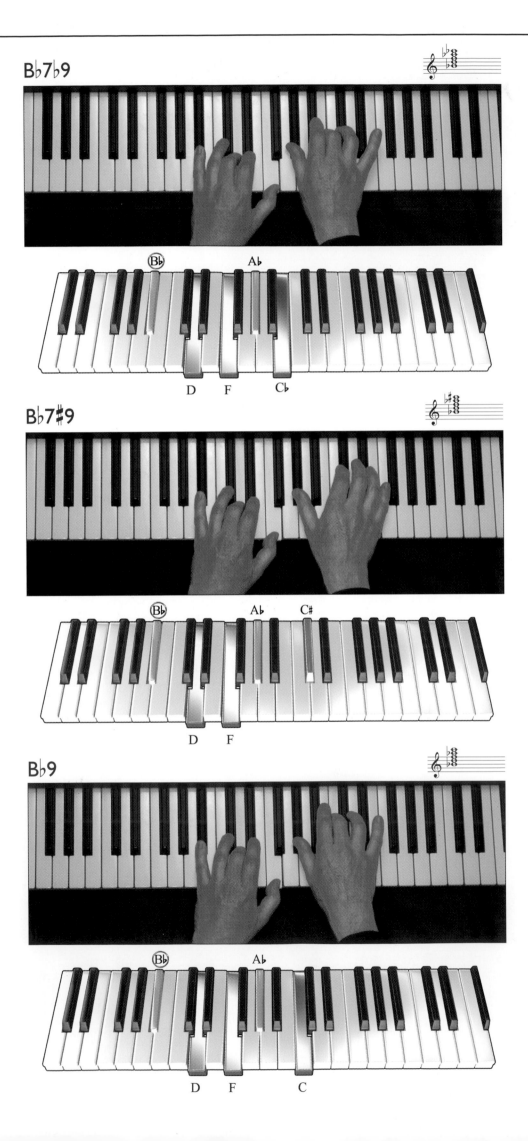

Bb7b9

Bb   Ab

D   F   Cb

Bb7#9

Bb   Ab   C#

D   F

Bb9

Bb   Ab

D   F   C

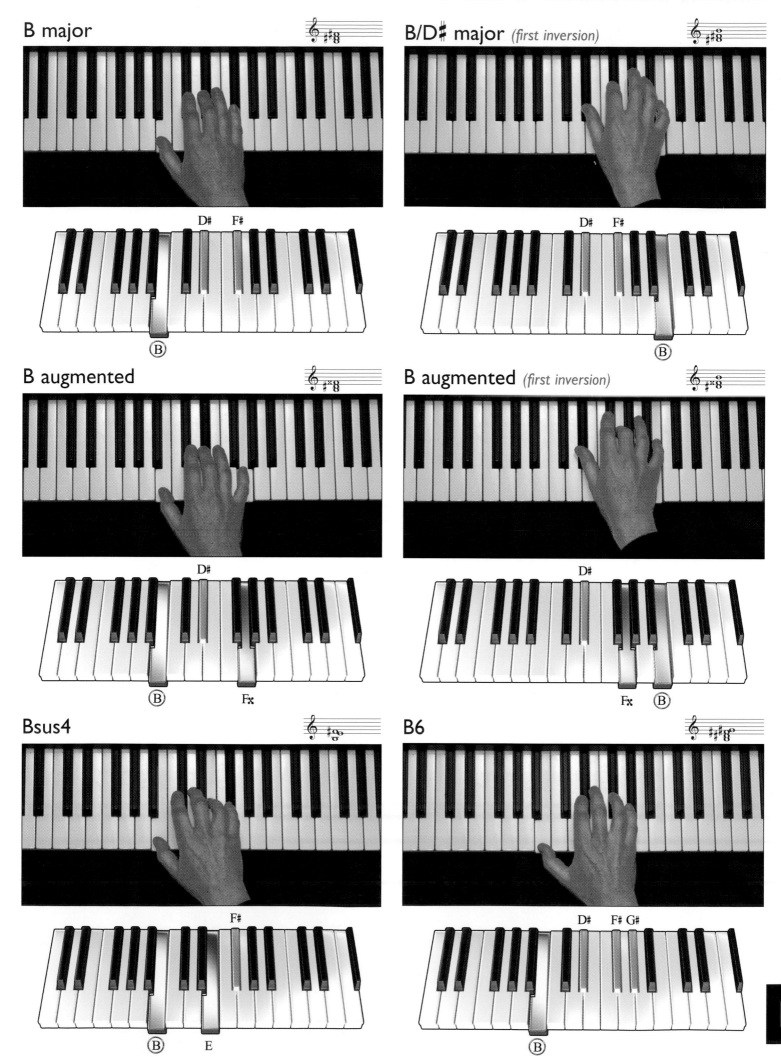

B major

B/D♯ major *(first inversion)*

D♯   F♯

Ⓑ

D♯   F♯

Ⓑ

B augmented

B augmented *(first inversion)*

D♯

Ⓑ   F𝕩

D♯

F𝕩   Ⓑ

Bsus4

B6

F♯

Ⓑ   E

D♯   F♯ G♯

Ⓑ

B

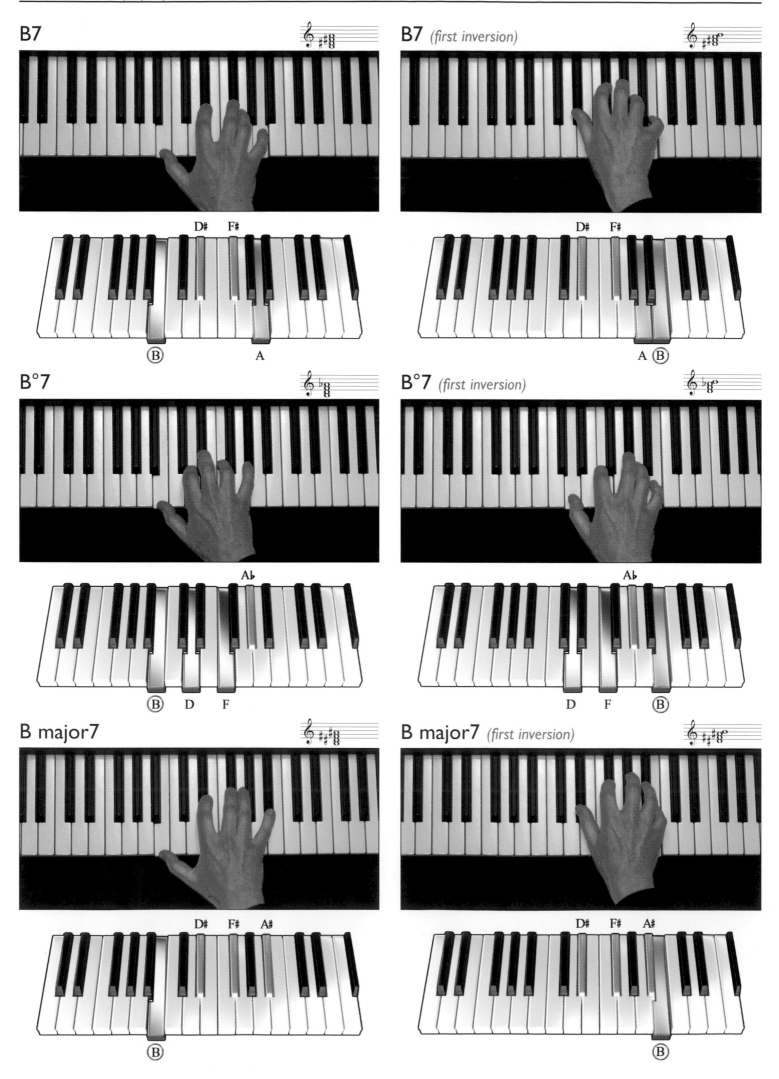

B7

D# F#

Ⓑ A

B7 *(first inversion)*

D# F#

A Ⓑ

B°7

A♭

Ⓑ D F

B°7 *(first inversion)*

A♭

D F Ⓑ

B major7

D# F# A#

Ⓑ

B major7 *(first inversion)*

D# F# A#

Ⓑ

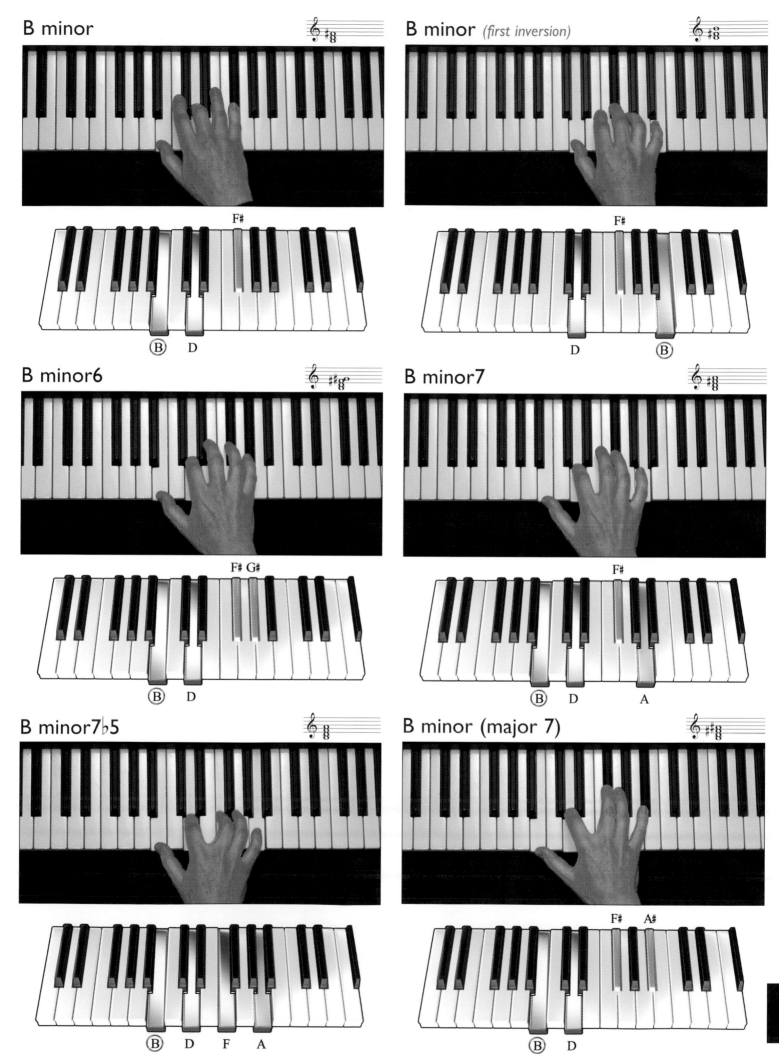

B minor

B minor *(first inversion)*

B minor6

B minor7

B minor7♭5

B minor (major 7)

B

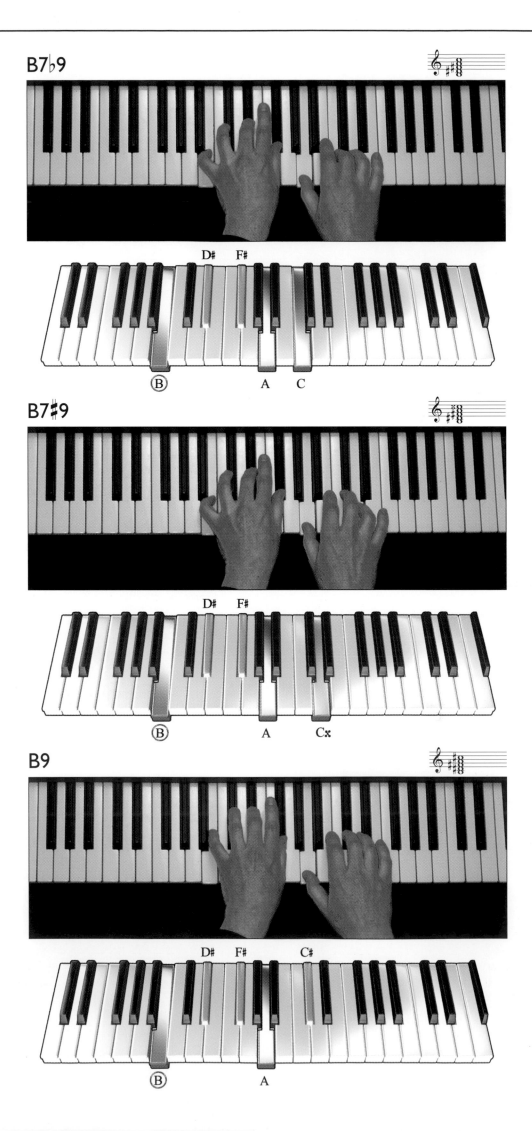

Chord Construction

Scales

In order to talk about chord structure we need to discuss the foundation by which chords are formed—*scales*. There are a multitude of scales available to the musician, but we will explain only those that are most pertinent— the major, minor, and chromatic scales.

Chromatic

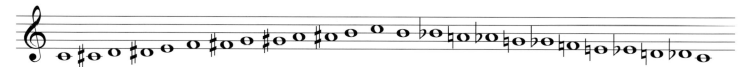

Major

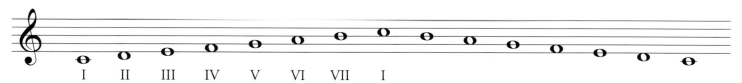

Harmonic minor

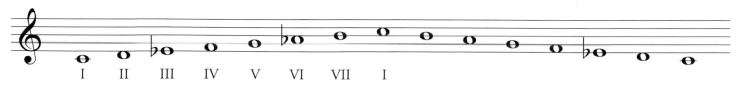

Melodic minor

Scales are determined by the distribution of half-tones and whole-tones. For example, the major scale has half-tones between scale steps three and four, and between seven and eight. The harmonic minor has half-tones between scale steps two and three, five and six, and seven and eight. The melodic minor scale's ascending order finds half-steps at six and five and three and two, and a whole-step is now in the place of eight and seven. It is common to refer to scale steps, or *degrees*, by Roman numerals as in the example above and also by the following names:

I.	Tonic
II.	Supertonic
III.	Mediant
IV.	Subdominant
V.	Dominant
VI.	Submediant
VII.	Leading-tone

Intervals

An *interval* is the distance between two notes. This is the basis for harmony (chords). The naming of intervals, as in the example below, is fairly standard, but you may encounter other terminology in various forms of musical literature.

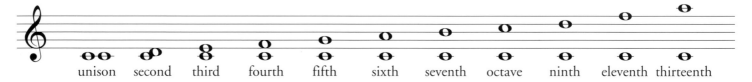

unison second third fourth fifth sixth seventh octave ninth eleventh thirteenth

Chords

Chords are produced by combining two or more intervals, and the simplest of these combinations is a *triad*. A triad consists of three notes obtained by the superposition of two thirds. The notes are called the *root*, the *third*, and the *fifth*.

fifth
third
root

Inversions

Inversions are produced by arranging the intervals of a chord in a different order. A triad that has the root as the bottom or lowest tone is said to be in *root position*. A triad with a third as the bottom or lowest tone is in *first* inversion, and a triad with a fifth as the bottom or lowest tone is in *second inversion*. As the chords become more complex—such as, sixths, sevenths, etc.—there will be more possible inversions.

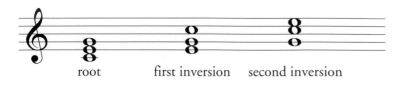

root   first inversion   second inversion

Note that when inverting more complex chords the inversion may actually become a completely different chord.

Altered Triads

When a chord consists of a root, major third, and a perfect fifth it is known as a *major* triad. When the triad is altered by lowering the major third one halfstep, it becomes a *minor* triad. The examples below are chords that have altered intervals.

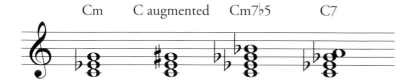

Enharmonic Spelling

Enharmonic tones are tones that have different notation or spelling, but have the same pitch; like C♯ and D♭. You will encounter these differences throughout this book, mostly as altered triads. The reason that this occurs is to make it easier to read while playing from a piece of music manuscript. In the following example, D♭m7♭9 demonstrates why this approach is practical and preferred. As stated before, triads are superposed thirds or notes that are stacked one on top of the other.

This allows the musician to see, at a glance, what chord they are going to play. So with this in mind, look at the D♭m7♭9 example. You will notice that the E♭ is double flatted (E♭♭), this allows the musician, again at a glance, to see that what would be the nine of the chord is now flatted. The other example is indeed the same chord, but by using the D instead of the E♭♭ the chord becomes harder to read.

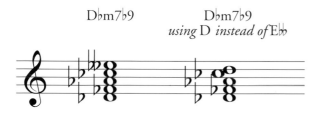

Alternate Chord Names

This chord book uses a standard chord-naming approach, but when playing from sheet music or using other music books, you will find alternative chord names or symbols. Below is a chart by which you can cross reference alternative names and symbols with the ones used in this book.

Chord Name	Alternate Name or Symbol
major	M; Maj
minor	m; min; -
6	Maj6; M6
minor6	min6; -6
6/9	6(add9); Maj6(add9); M6(add9)
major7	M7; Maj7; Δ7; Δ
7	dominant seventh; dom
7♭5	7(♭5); 7(-5)
7♯5	+7; 7(+5); aug7
minor7	m7; min7; -7
minor (major7)	m(M7); min(Maj7); m(+7); -(M7); min(addM7)
minor7♭5	∅7; ½dim; ½dim7; m7(♭5); m7(-5)
°7	°; dim; dim7
9	7(add9)
9♭5	9(♭5); 9(-5)
9♯5	+9; 9(+5); aug9
major9	M9; Δ9; Maj7(add9); M7(add9)
7♭9	7(♭9); 7(add♭9); 7-9; -9
minor11	m11; min11
♯11	(+11); Δ(+11); M7(+11); Δ(♯11); M7(♯11)
13	7(add13); 7(add6)
major13	M13; Δ(add13); Maj7(add13); M7(add13); M7(add6)
minor13	m13; -13; min7(add13); m7(add13); -7 (add13);
sus4	(sus4)
augmented	aug; (♯5); +5